WIT

"Rachel has now made it possible for healthy meals to fit into a busy lifestyle for the average American family. This cookbook is a new essential for all level of cooks as it provides a variety of recipes for every palate. A must-buy for any person wanting to maintain a delicious and healthy diet."

—Liz Stambaugh, President of Slow Food Baltimore

"A variety of dishes from around the world including Chinese, Italian, French, Korean, Indian, and regional American cuisines makes slow cooking fun and interesting again! A focus on spices and fresh ingredients means these recipes are as full of flavor as they are healthful."

—Monica Bhide, Author of *Modern Spice* and *The Everything® Indian Cookbook*

"Rachel's approach to the kitchen is insanely genuine. I appreciate her respect toward the ingredients she uses and I believe in her recipes when I read them. This book will come back with me to Tuscany! If I did not know that this was Rachel's book, I would think it was written by a very wise and knowledgeable Italian woman that has traveled a bit! I was cooking spaghetti with pesto tonight, then I started reading Rachel's book. Now I am frantically browsing my cabinets and fridge to see which one of her recipes I can prepare."

—Gabriele Corcos, Co-host of Tuscan cooking show *Under the Tuscan Gun* (*www.underthetuscangun.com*)

"Who says you can't get great flavor and healthy meals out of a slow cooker? *The Everything® Healthy Slow Cooker Cookbook* is a boon to families, couples, and anyone trying to eat better without a lot of effort."

—Amy Sherman, Author of *Williams-Sonoma New Flavors for Appetizers*

THE
EVERYTHING
HEALTHY SLOW COOKER
COOKBOOK

Dear Reader,

In this book I strove to include a variety of recipes from many different cuisines as well as healthier versions of old favorites. I hope this book inspires you to use your slow cooker more often and in new ways. Slow cooking doesn't have to mean heavy meat dishes and cream of mushroom soup! Dishes using lean meats, fresh fruits, and vegetables can be made easily and deliciously in the slow cooker. Fresh ingredients and wonderful spices yield food that is tasty as well as healthful.

While many people have a tendency to use the slow cooker more in the colder months, I find myself reaching for it frequently during the summer and spring. It doesn't heat up the house as much as using the oven or range does. Here you will find many recipes that use seasonal produce, and I think you will find yourself using the slow cooker all year long.

Rachel Rappaport

Welcome to the **EVERYTHING**® Series!

These handy, accessible books give you all you need to tackle a difficult project, gain a new hobby, comprehend a fascinating topic, prepare for an exam, or even brush up on something you learned back in school but have since forgotten.

You can choose to read an Everything® book from cover to cover or just pick out the information you want from our four useful boxes: e-questions, e-facts, e-alerts, and e-ssentials.

We give you everything you need to know on the subject, but throw in a lot of fun stuff along the way, too.

We now have more than 400 Everything® books in print, spanning such wide-ranging categories as weddings, pregnancy, cooking, music instruction, foreign language, crafts, pets, New Age, and so much more. When you're done reading them all, you can finally say you know Everything®!

QUESTION
Answers to
common questions

FACT
Important snippets
of information

ALERT
Urgent
warnings

ESSENTIAL
Quick
handy tips

PUBLISHER Karen Cooper

DIRECTOR OF ACQUISITIONS AND INNOVATION Paula Munier

MANAGING EDITOR, EVERYTHING® SERIES Lisa Laing

COPY CHIEF Casey Ebert

ACQUISITIONS EDITOR Katrina Schroeder

ASSOCIATE DEVELOPMENT EDITOR Hillary Thompson

EDITORIAL ASSISTANT Ross Weisman

EVERYTHING® SERIES COVER DESIGNER Erin Alexander

LAYOUT DESIGNERS Colleen Cunningham, Elisabeth Lariviere, Ashley Vierra, Denise Wallace

Visit the entire Everything® series at *www.everything.com*

THE
EVERYTHING®
HEALTHY SLOW COOKER COOKBOOK

Rachel Rappaport with B. E. Horton, MS, RD

Avon, Massachusetts

To my beloved Grandpop, who inspired
a lifelong love of cooking.

An Everything® Series Book.
Everything® and everything.com® are registered trademarks of F+W Media, Inc.

Published by Adams Media, a division of F+W Media, Inc.
57 Littlefield Street, Avon, MA 02322 U.S.A.
www.adamsmedia.com

ISBN 10: 1-4405-0231-5
ISBN 13: 978-1-4405-0231-6
eISBN 10: 1-4405-0232-3
eISBN 13: 978-1-4405-0232-3

Printed in the United States of America.

10 9 8 7 6 5 4 3 2 1

Library of Congress Cataloging-in-Publication Data
Rappaport, Rachel.
The everything healthy slow cooker cookbook / Rachel Rappaport with B.E. Horton.
p. cm.—(Everything)
ISBN 978-1-4405-0231-6
1. Electric cookery, Slow. 2. Low-carbohydrate diet—Recipes. 3. Nutrition. I. Horton, B. E. II. Title.
TX827.R28   2010
641.5'884—dc22   2010009947

This book is available at quantity discounts for bulk purchases.
For information, please call 1-800-289-0963.

Contents

Acknowledgments

I would like to thank my husband, Matt, who is always supportive of me and my endeavors. He was incredibly helpful during the recipe development process. I would also like to thank all of the family and friends who happily came over for slow-cooked meals and who devoured the copious leftovers from recipe experiments. I truly appreciate it.

Introduction

FOR YEARS SLOW COOKERS have been associated with heavy, rich dishes that are anything but healthy. While these dishes might be tasty and are fine for an occasional treat, for every day, some healthier recipes are needed. Luckily, it is as easy to make a healthy meal in the slow cooker as it is to make an unhealthy one. Making simple ingredient substitutions and choosing recipes that are high on flavor, fruits, fiber, vegetables, and lean protein instead of fat are the keys to healthy slow-cooking success.

Meals can be assembled in the morning and eaten immediately upon arrival home. It is even faster than getting takeout! Healthy alternatives to traditional heavy soup and canned-good slow cooker recipes are perfect for people who like modern, creative food similar to what would be served in a restaurant. These recipes are easy to follow and include ingredients that can be found in almost any supermarket.

Healthy eating means choosing foods for optimal health. Recipes that use whole grains, fresh fruits and vegetables, lean meats, and fiber-rich legumes go a long way toward promoting a healthy autoimmune system and digestive tract. The trick is to use foods that are high in flavor but not fat. Using fruits, vegetables, and spices to flavor a meal instead of rich sauces is a step in the right direction. Fresh ingredients like onions, garlic, fennel, celery, carrots, apples, pears, and mangoes add lots of flavor, are low in calories, and are high in fiber.

Eating healthily does not mean giving up entirely on old favorites, just learning how to prepare them in a new, more wholesome way. There is no reason to use high-sodium and calorific condensed soups when fat-free evaporated milk adds creaminess without the fat. Spices add richness and robust flavor while adding virtually no calories. Very lean cuts of meat will become tender after cooking for hours. Making biscuit and dumpling toppings from scratch saves calories, and these recipes are just as easy as using a mix. The slow cooker can also be used to create flavorful yet low-fat stocks and sauces that can be used in many other recipes instead of bottled or canned alternatives.

Slow cooking isn't just for dinner! Breakfast can easily be made in the slow cooker. Egg dishes are a wonderful way to start your day with lots of protein. Whole-grain cereals cook overnight so you can wake up to a hot, high-fiber, filling breakfast with no work required. Or try a dessert that is cooking while you eat dinner. Even appetizers, dips, sauces, and spreads can be made with minimal effort in the slow cooker. It truly is an all-day, all-year appliance.

In this book you will find 300 recipes to choose from based on calorie count, fiber content, fat content, and nutritional profile. Some recipes are "slimmed-down" versions of old favorites while others are fresh new ways to consume healthful foods with little effort. The recipes are all so full-flavored that you won't miss the extra fat and calories found in most other slow cooker dishes. The wide range of regional and international choices will suit large families, couples, vegetarians, vegans, and dessert lovers.

CHAPTER 1

Cooking Healthy Meals
in the Slow Cooker

Coming home to a delicious, home-cooked meal is the perfect end to a hard day of work or a busy day running errands. Luckily, it is easy to do just that when you use your slow cooker. This chapter will guide you through the process of becoming adept at making flavorful, healthful meals in your slow cooker. Learn about the benefits of slow cooking, the various types of slow cookers, slow cooker–friendly ingredients, and even how to convert some of your favorite recipes into slow cooker recipes.

The Benefits of Slow Cooking

The benefits of slow cooking are numerous. Slow cookers can be used to make main dishes, one-pot meals, side dishes, even desserts. Most recipes call for a few minutes of prep time and zero hands-on time during the actual cooking. For a small amount of effort in the morning, you can come home to a hot meal after a full workday. The recipes with shorter cooking times are perfect for those instances when space and time are limited when you're running errands, throwing a party, or trying to fit in a meal during the holidays.

The long cooking times associated with most slow cooker recipes mean that cheaper, leaner cuts of meat come out just as tender as a $30 well-marbled steak. You can turn affordable root vegetables into mouthwatering soups, stews, and side dishes with minimal effort. You can also make pantry staples such as homemade stocks, barbecue sauce, pasta sauces, and even granola for mere pennies in the slow cooker.

While slow cookers are closely associated with wintertime stews, soups, and roasts, they are wonderful to use year-round. Since they do not heat the house the way oven or stovetop cooking does, slow cookers are perfect for warm weather, too. In-season fruits and vegetables at the peak of their flavor and nutritional value make excellent additions to slow cooker dishes.

FACT

The Rival Corporation introduced slow cookers in 1970. In 1974 Rival began selling the removable ceramic insert, which made cleaning the slow cooker easier and safer. Since 1970 over 80 million slow cookers have been sold.

Although cooking on the grill or stovetop may be faster, it requires a lot more hands-on time and attention. A piece of meat left cooking in a skillet unattended will burn. Soups or sauces left unstirred will thicken, burn, and stick to the pot. These are not issues that occur with a slow cooker. Since a slow cooker uses low, indirect heat, there is no reason to stir or watch the food as it cooks. In fact, there is virtually no risk of burning food in the slow cooker, which makes it a perfect fit for the busy or distracted cook.

Healthy Choices

It is quite easy to make healthy food in the slow cooker. Very little oil or fat is needed because keeping ingredients from sticking to the cooker is not an issue. Since liquids do not evaporate in the slow cooker, very lean meats will not dry out or overcook the way they might on the stovetop or grill, leaving them amazingly tender. Additionally, using lean meats ensures that your chili, soup, or roast won't be unappetizingly greasy.

Whole grains like oatmeal, wheat berries, barley, rice, and corn are all well suited to use in the slow cooker. A variety of dishes incorporate nuts and seeds, a wonderful way to introduce healthy fats and fiber into your diet. High-fiber fruits, vegetables and legumes are at the center of most slow cooker meals.

Types and Sizes of Slow Cookers

Slow cookers have come a long way from their avocado green, one-size-fits-all days. Now they're available in several sizes and with many modern features. The small 1½- to 2-quart slow cooker is perfect for smaller families and couples. The 4-quart cooker, the most popular size, is capable of making meals that serve four to six people. The largest models are 6–7 quarts and can feed a crowd of eight or more. Hamilton Beach manufactures a three-in-one slow cooker that comes with a set of 2-, 4-, and 6-quart ceramic inserts that can be used one at a time in the same base, eliminating the need to own multiple slow cookers.

Settling on Settings

Look for slow cookers that have at least a low and high setting. This is standard for the mid- to large-size models, but many 2-quart models only have an on/off option. Temperature control is essential if you make full meals in a small slow cooker. Slow cookers equipped solely with an on/off switch are suitable only for keeping fondues, dips, or beverages warm.

ESSENTIAL

You can check that your slow cooker is cooking food to the proper temperature by conducting a simple test. Fill the slow cooker two-thirds of the way with water. Cover and cook on low for 8 hours. The temperature of the water at the end of the cooking time should be 185°F. If it is not, replace your slow cooker.

Lifestyle Choices

It is important to choose a slow cooker with features that fit your lifestyle. Many slow cookers have a warm setting that will keep your food warm at approximately 160°F. This setting may be manual, but if the slow cooker is digital, it will automatically turn on after the programmed cooking time has finished. The automatic switch to warm is especially helpful for people who are not sure when they will have dinner. If you enjoy cooking large cuts of meat, look for a model that comes with a probe thermometer that takes an exact temperature of the food inside. Once the meat reaches the desired temperature, the slow cooker will switch to warm to avoid overcooking. If you plan to take your slow cooker to parties or potlucks, there are several models that have secure latches to hold the lid on while in transit. Some models made for travel come with built-in serving spoon holders and rests. There are also models that have an insulated case for the stoneware insert. If cutting down on the number of dirty dishes is important, look for a slow cooker that has an insert that can be placed on top of the stove. Those inserts can brown meats and vegetables and can be put back in the base to finish cooking.

Shape Matters

For most recipes, you can use either an oval or a round slow cooker. However, for roasts, meatloaf, or lasagna, or for slow-cooking large pieces of fish, an oval cooker is preferable because it allows the food to lie flat.

What is the difference between a slow cooker and a Crock Pot?
Crock Pots and slow cookers are the same thing. Although the term
Crock Pot is frequently used generically, it is actually a registered
trademark for a specific brand of slow cooker. Various brands of cookers may vary in appearance and features but all function essentially the
same way.

The Perfect Ingredients

Nearly any food works well in the slow cooker, but certain ingredients are
especially well suited to slow cooking.

Canned Goods

Evaporated milk is shelf-stable canned milk, which is made by removing 60 percent of the water from regular milk. When mixed with an equal
amount of water, evaporated milk becomes the equivalent of fresh milk.
Rehydration is often unnecessary in slow cooking. Using the evaporated
milk straight from the can is a great way to add a creamy, dairy flavor without the fat. Unlike fresh milk, evaporated milk is safe to use in recipes with
long cooking times without fear of curdling.

Canned beans are precooked and recipe-ready unlike dried beans,
which still need to be soaked and fully cooked before being added to the
slow cooker. Beans are a wonderful source of protein and fiber and are virtually fat free. Be sure to drain and rinse canned beans prior to use. You can
substitute cooked, rehydrated dried beans equally for canned.

Canned tomatoes are better tasting than out-of-season fresh tomatoes.
Unless otherwise noted, add the juice to the slow cooker along with the
tomatoes. It can add much-needed moisture to a dish without having to add
water or broth.

Produce

Onions are essential to many slow cooking recipes. Due to their high
moisture content, onions give off a lot of liquid as they cook. Instead of

adding water or broth to a recipe, which can dilute the flavor of the dish, try onions to provide both moisture and flavor. Onions are especially useful when cooking large cuts of meat or other dishes where you want a drier final product.

Root vegetables such as carrots, parsnips, beets, celeriac, rutabaga, turnips, and potatoes are exceptionally suited to the slow cooker because they retain their shape and texture even after being cooked for hours. Peel carrots, beets, rutabaga, turnips, and parsnips before using them. Potatoes can be used peeled or unpeeled.

Corn, broccoli, cabbage, snow peas, green beans, apples, pears, mangoes, figs, cranberries, strawberries, raspberries, blackberries, blueberries, and tomatoes are all suitable for slow cooking and are high in dietary fiber, which is essential to digestive tract health.

ALERT

Vegetables can lose valuable nutrients during long cooking times. Blanching the vegetables by cooking them briefly in boiling water helps them retain vitamins. Sautéing vegetables prior to adding them to the slow cooker also optimizes nutrient retention.

Stock Tips

Stock—whether beef, chicken, turkey, vegetable, or seafood—can be used instead of water in almost any dish made in the slow cooker. Recipes made with stock are more flavorful than those made with water. For best results, use salt-free, fat-free stock.

Cooking with Meat

Lean cuts of meat are perfect for the slow cooker. The long cooking time tenderizes the meat, leaving it fork tender. Additionally, using lean meat in dishes like chili is necessary because it's not possible to skim off the fat after cooking. When cooking with beef, look for the least marbled cuts; choose lean cuts such as tri-tip, top or bottom round roast, top sirloin, or flat half-brisket, all of which meet the governmental standards for very lean or lean meats. When shopping for pork, look for pork tenderloin, boneless pork loin chop, and boneless pork top loin, all of which contain less than 5 percent fat per serving. Boneless, skinless chicken breasts and thighs are also great sources of lean protein. Most grocery stores carry 94 percent lean ground chicken, turkey, pork, and beef.

ESSENTIAL

Food that is similar in size will cook at the same time. For soups and stews, cut the meat and vegetables into uniformly sized pieces to ensure that they will be fully cooked at the same time. When cooking large cuts of meat, leave the vegetables in large chunks to avoid overcooking.

Adapting Standard Recipes

Although there are many recipes for the slow cooker, you can never have too many. Converting regular recipes to be made in the slow cooker can be a rewarding experience. Long simmering, braising, stewing, and slow roasting recipes, most of which require more than one hour cooking time on the stove top or oven, can be converted in a slow cooker recipe. The slow cooker recipe will require far less hands-on time and will have similar (or identical) final products. The most successful converted recipes require the majority of the work in the preparation. While some ingredients can be added to the slow cooker toward the end of the cooking time, recipes that are labor-intensive or that require many steps may not be well suited to this method.

Understanding how a slow cooker works will help you successfully adapt your recipes. Slow cookers have a ceramic insert that is surrounded by a heating element; this configuration keeps the temperature inside constant. The lid contains the heat and moisture so there is little evaporation. Temperatures can vary depending on the age and model of the slow cooker, but as a general rule, the low setting is 170°F and high is 200°F. Food cooked on low takes roughly twice as long as food cooked on high.

Soups and Stews

The easiest type of recipe to convert is a soup or stew. Follow the preparation of the original recipe but leave out ingredients such as cooked poultry, rice, pasta, or quinoa and stop short of simmering. Add any browned meats, vegetables, and broth to the slow cooker and cook on low for 8 hours. Add the poultry, rice, pasta, or quinoa during the last 30 minutes of cooking to avoid overcooking them. The lack of evaporation and constant heat ensures stews that will never dry out and soups that cook without boiling over or evaporating.

QUESTION

Can I use the slow cooker to cook seafood?
Seafood can be cooked in the slow cooker, but use caution because seafood can easily overcook. Most seafood should be added during the last 15 to 30 minutes of cooking. The only exception is an oily fish like salmon, which can be cooked up to 2 hours on low with no ill effect. In fact, the fish will be amazingly tender and moist due to the lack of evaporation.

Liquid Assets

Although a lack of evaporation is not an issue when it comes to cooking soups, the amount of liquid in most recipes needs to be reduced when adjusting them for the slow cooker. Regular recipes assume some liquid will evaporate during the cooking time. Additionally, some ingredients such as onions, meats, peppers, and tomatoes give off a lot of liquid as they slow-cook. It is better to err on the side of caution and at least halve the amount of liquid in a traditional recipe. If after slow cooking too much liquid is left, you can still save the dish. For a small amount of excess liquid, remove the lid of the slow cooker and cook on high for 30 minutes to allow for some evaporation. If a lot of liquid remains, drain it off and reduce it in a pot on the stove.

Meat

Meat does not brown in the slow cooker. If you want browning for flavor or aesthetic reasons, you need to brown the meat before adding it to the slow cooker. Quickly searing meat in a dry skillet or sautéing it can accomplish this. For stews that need a thicker broth, toss the meat in flour prior to sautéing to help with both browning and thickening. Slow cooking is perfect for recipes that call for cheaper, leaner cuts of meat that need a long cooking time to become tender. For best results, surround the meat with carrots, celery, fennel, or raw or caramelized onions, which will provide the necessary moisture and flavor.

If the original recipe calls for a high-fat cut of meat, substitute a leaner cut. High-fat meats are not well suited to the slow cooker because they become greasy and tough. For example, instead of using bone-in pork shoulder, use pork tenderloin.

Boneless cuts of chicken, turkey, or duck cook relatively quickly in the slow cooker; do not cook them for longer than 4 hours on low or 2 hours on high. Boneless poultry works best in the slow cooker when it is paired with wet ingredients such as sauces, tomatoes, or soft fruit. This insures that the lean meat will not dry out during the cooking time.

ALERT

Keep perishable items refrigerated until it is time to add them to the slow cooker. Cutting up ingredients the night before can save time, but they should be kept covered and refrigerated until ready for use. Additionally, store cut up meat and vegetables in separate containers to avoid cross-contamination.

Dairy Dos and Don'ts

Dairy products, like sour cream, cream cheese, or milk, do not hold up well over long cooking times. To avoid curdling, add them during the last half hour of cooking. If you are making a hot dip, do not heat it for more than an hour unless otherwise instructed. If milk is a major ingredient, for example, in a creamy sauce or soup, substitute an equal amount of evaporated milk. Evaporated milk can be used directly from the can, and since it has been heat-processed, it can withstand long cooking times. Due to the relatively short, low-heat cooking time of the last half hour, low-fat sour cream, cream cheese, or milk can be used with great success in the slow cooker despite having a tendency to separate while cooked using traditional methods.

Keep It Spicy

Experimenting with different flavor combinations is part of the fun of slow cooking. It is also a wonderful way to add flavor to a dish without adding fat. You can use herbs and spices in the same amounts as you would with other cooking methods. Using fresh spices is essential. As spices age, they lose their potency. Taste what you are making before you serve it. If the finished dish is too bland, stir in additional spices prior to serving. Adding soft vegetables such as fresh or frozen peas and corn during the last 30 to 60 minutes of cooking is another way to perk up the flavor of a dish.

ESSENTIAL

Most savory recipes can be cooked on low for 8 hours to no ill effect. When in doubt, cook a recipe on low. It is virtually impossible to overcook food in the slow cooker. However, if the food is not fully cooked at the end of the cooking time, turning the temperature to high can help speed up the cooking process.

Pantry Essentials

Keeping a well-stocked pantry is essential. Having basic yet versatile ingredients on hand makes it easy to make a home-cooked meal on the spur of the moment.

Cabinet Staples

Recipes from a wide range of cuisines incorporate canned goods such as fat-free evaporated milk, fat-free sweetened condensed milk, black beans, kidney beans, cannellini beans, black olives, crushed tomatoes, whole tomatoes, tomato paste, and diced tomatoes. Look for low-sodium versions to help reduce your salt intake. Keeping these canned goods on hand will enable you to throw together a delicious, nutritious meal at the last minute.

Stock sold in cartons is generally better tasting than canned and does not need to be refrigerated until opened. Although it is not as tasty as homemade stock, it is helpful to have a few cartons on hand. Buy fat-free, salt-free stock.

Small pastas like orzo, acini di pepe, pastina, alfabeto, and ditalini are perfect for adding to soups. Look for whole-wheat versions for added fiber.

All-purpose flour, cornmeal, baking powder, canola oil, olive oil, wheat berries, barley, and oatmeal are all great in the slow cooker and they have long shelf lives. Additionally, dried fruits and sun-dried tomatoes can be kept on hand to toss in a dish for extra flavor and fiber.

International Cooking Made Easy

Cans of chipotle in adobo, chopped green chiles, hot sauces, and tomatoes with green chiles are all shelf stable. Keep them on hand for making chili, tortilla soup, tamale pie, and other spicy Mexican dishes.

Fish sauce, dark and light soy sauce, chili-garlic sauce, rice vinegar, rice noodles, sesame oil, and Chinese cooking wine can be found in most well-stocked grocery stores. These ingredients are indispensable in many pan-Asian recipes.

Spice It Up

A well-stocked spice cabinet is essential for making tasty slow cooker dishes. Chipotle powder, paprika, black pepper, chili powder, ground jalapeño, hot Mexican chili powder, and cayenne pepper can add heat and a depth of flavor to almost any dish. Dried herbs such as oregano, celery flakes, chervil, thyme, rosemary, dill weed, and parsley add a lot of flavor and have a long shelf life. Aromatic spices including cloves, cumin, allspice, nutmeg, cinnamon, and cocoa can be used in savory or sweet dishes. Additional spices that are used less frequently but are still helpful to have around include fennel seed, fenugreek, sumac, mustard seeds, garlic powder, onion powder, diced onion, dill seed, caraway seed, and Chesapeake Bay seasoning.

Storing Other Ingredients

While not technically pantry ingredients, ground meats, chicken breasts and thighs, pork chops, cooked chicken or turkey, and salmon freeze well and can be defrosted in the refrigerator overnight. Minced fresh herbs can be frozen and used directly from the freezer in any recipe that calls for fresh herbs.

Properly stored in cool, dark places, potatoes, apples, parsnips, rutabagas, and winter squash can last an entire season. Stock up and have them on hand at all times for easy yet flavorful meals.

Slow-Cooking Tips

The first time you use a slow cooker, it is helpful to be home to check in on the dish to see how it is cooking. Some slow cookers may run hotter or cooler than others, and it is important to know whether the cooking time needs to be adjusted. Additionally, you don't want to come home to a cold, raw meal because the slow cooker did not turn on or work properly.

Slow cookers work best when they are at least one-half to two-thirds full. Less food will cook more quickly and less evenly. Choose a slow cooker that is the proper size for the recipe for best results.

Pay attention to layering instructions. Place slower-cooking ingredients like root vegetables near the bottom of the slow cooker unless otherwise noted.

Remove any visible fat from meat before adding it to the slow cooker. Also be sure to drain off any rendered fat before putting browned meat in the slow cooker.

Safety First

Heating an empty ceramic insert may cause it to crack. Be sure the insert is at room temperature when placed in the slow cooker base. Sudden changes in temperature can also cause cracks in the ceramic insert.

Defrost all frozen meats in the refrigerator before placing them in the slow cooker. The food in the slow cooker must reach the safe temperature of 140°F as soon as possible. Using frozen meat may lower the temperature of the dish into the danger zone for an extended period. Small frozen vegetables like peas or corn will not lower the temperature enough to be dangerous but add them toward the end of the cooking time for best texture and flavor.

To keep the temperature constant in the slow cooker, avoid removing the lid during the cooking time. Removing the lid can reduce the temperature in the cooker, adding to the overall cooking time. Additionally, do not repeatedly add new items to the slow cooker during the cooking process. It can cause the internal temperature to dip below what is considered safe. If additional ingredients need to be added, they should be added all at once toward the end of the cooking time.

ALERT

Refrigerate leftovers within 2 hours of finishing cooking. It is not safe to keep the food warm in the slow cooker indefinitely. Serving utensils can introduce bacteria to the food that will not be killed off by the low temperatures of the warm setting. Reheat leftovers in the oven, stovetop, or microwave.

The outside of some slow cookers can become quite hot. Do not place flammable items or items that may melt near the slow cooker while it is in use. All modern slow cookers have short cords to reduce the risk of tipping over, but it is still important to keep them away from small children and pets. Contents in the slow cooker can be near boiling temperatures and the hot exteriors can cause burns or skin irritation.

CHAPTER 2

Slow Cooker Foundation Recipes

Caramelized Onions

Caramelized onions are a great addition to roasts, dips, and sandwiches.

INGREDIENTS | YIELDS 1 QUART

4 pounds Vidalia or other sweet onions
3 tablespoons butter
1 tablespoon balsamic vinegar

Storing Caramelized Onions

Store the onions in an airtight container. They will keep up to 2 weeks refrigerated or up to 6 months frozen. If frozen, defrost overnight in the refrigerator before using.

1. Peel and slice the onions in ¼" slices. Separate them into rings. Thinly slice the butter.

2. Place the onions into a 4-quart slow cooker. Scatter butter slices over top of the onions and drizzle with balsamic vinegar. Cover and cook on low for 10 hours.

3. If after 10 hours the onions are wet, turn the slow cooker up to high and cook uncovered for an additional 30 minutes or until the liquid evaporates.

PER 2 TABLESPOONS Calories: 35 | Fat: 1g | Sodium: 0mg | Carbohydrates: 6g | Fiber: <1g | Protein: 1g

Corn on the Cob

This is a great way to have hot corn on the cob without having to heat up the kitchen during the summer months. After cooking, turn the slow cooker to warm and let everyone help themselves!

INGREDIENTS | SERVES 6

6 ears corn, husks removed
½ teaspoon salt
Water, as needed

Place the corn in the bottom of an oval 4-quart slow cooker. Sprinkle in the salt. Fill the insert with water until the water level is 1" below the top. Cover and cook for 5 hours on low or 2 on high.

PER SERVING Calories: 80 | Fat: 1g | Sodium: 210mg | Carbohydrates: 17g | Fiber: 2g | Protein: 3g

Chicken Stock

Homemade chicken stock is much cheaper and tastier than store-bought.

INGREDIENTS | **YIELDS 3 QUARTS**

1 chicken carcass

2 carrots, cut into chunks

2 stalks celery, cut into chunks

2 onions, cut into chunks

2 parsnips, cut into chunks

1 head garlic

2 chicken wings

Water, as needed

Stock Options

Any leftover vegetables can be added to stock for extra flavor; fennel fronds, green onions, turnips, and red onion are all good choices. Depending on the recipe that the stock will be used in, adding items like dried chiles, ginger, or galangal root will customize the stock, making it an even better fit for the final product.

1. Place the carcass, carrots, celery, onions, parsnips, garlic, and wings into a 6-quart slow cooker.

2. Fill the slow cooker with water until it is 2" below the top. Cover and cook on low for 10 hours.

3. Strain into a large container. Discard the solids. Refrigerate the stock overnight.

4. The next day, scoop off any fat that has floated to the top. Discard the fat.

5. Freeze or refrigerate the broth until ready to use.

PER 1 CUP Calories: 60 | Fat: 1.5g | Sodium: 25mg | Carbohydrates: 10g | Fiber: 2g | Protein: 3g

Corn Bread

Corn bread is the perfect accompaniment to chili or soup.

INGREDIENTS | **SERVES 8**

1½ cups stone-ground cornmeal

¾ cup all-purpose flour

1 cup fat-free evaporated milk

1 tablespoon sugar

¼ teaspoon salt

1 cup fresh corn kernels

3½ tablespoons canola oil

2 eggs

Nonstick cooking spray, as needed

1. In a medium bowl, whisk together all ingredients except the cooking spray. Spray a 4-quart round slow cooker with nonstick cooking spray.

2. Pour the batter into the slow cooker and cook on high for 2 hours. Slice the corn bread and lift out the slices.

PER SERVING Calories: 280 | Fat: 9g | Sodium: 130mg | Carbohydrates: 43g | Fiber: 3g | Protein: 8g

A Bit about Corn Bread

Corn bread is a generic name for quick breads made with cornmeal. In the Northern states, corn bread is generally sweet and made with yellow cornmeal. In the South, corn bread is traditionally unsweetened and made with white cornmeal.

Roasted Vegetable Stock

*Use this in vegetarian recipes as a substitute for chicken stock
or in other recipes as a flavorful alternative to water.*

INGREDIENTS | YIELDS 5 QUARTS

3 carrots, peeled

3 parsnips, peeled

3 large onions, quartered

3 whole turnips

3 rutabagas, quartered

3 bell peppers, halved

2 shallots

1 whole head garlic

1 bunch fresh thyme

1 bunch parsley

5 quarts water

1. Preheat oven to 425°F. Arrange the vegetables and herbs in a 9" x 13" baking pan lined with parchment paper. Roast for 30 minutes or until browned.

2. Add the vegetables to a 6-quart slow cooker. Add 5 quarts of water and cover. Cook on low for 8–10 hours. Strain the stock, discarding the solids. Freeze or refrigerate the stock until ready to use.

PER 1 CUP Calories: 100 | Fat: 0g | Sodium: 45mg | Carbohydrates: 24g | Fiber: 5g | Protein: 3g

Poached Chicken

*Use moist, tender poached chicken in any recipe that calls for cooked
chicken. It is especially good in salads and sandwiches.*

INGREDIENTS | SERVES 8

4–5 pounds whole chicken or chicken parts

1 carrot, peeled

1 stalk celery

1 onion, quartered

1 cup water

1. Place the chicken into an oval 6-quart slow cooker. Arrange the vegetables around the chicken. Add the water. Cook on low for 7–8 hours.

2. Remove the skin before eating.

PER SERVING Calories: 330 | Fat: 8g | Sodium: 220mg | Carbohydrates: 3g | Fiber: <1g | Protein: 58g

Quick Chicken Salad

Stir together 2 cups cubed poached chicken breast, 3 tablespoons mayonnaise, ¼ cup diced celery, 1 minced shallot, and ¼ cup dried cranberries. Refrigerate for 1 hour. Serve on multigrain crackers or whole-wheat rolls.

Spicy Smoked Turkey Stock

Use this to add a smoky, spicy kick to any recipe that calls for water or any kind of stock.

INGREDIENTS | **YIELDS 3½ QUARTS**

2 smoked turkey drumsticks

5 dried guajillo chiles, stems and seeds removed

5 dried pasilla chiles, stems and seeds removed

6 dried red chiles, stems and seeds removed

3½ quarts water

1 large onion, quartered

3 cloves garlic

1. Place all ingredients into a 4-quart slow cooker. Cook on low for 10 hours.

2. Strain the liquid through a fine-mesh sieve, and discard the solids. Refrigerate overnight.

3. The next day, skim off any fat that has floated to the surface. Refrigerate or freeze the stock until needed.

PER 1 CUP Calories: 90 | Fat: 3.5g | Sodium: 330mg | Carbohydrates: 4g | Fiber: <1g | Protein: 10g

Stock Tips

Homemade stock tastes so much better than anything you can find in a can. However, it can be overwhelming to be faced with 3 or more quarts of stock at one time. Freeze it in recipe-ready quantities such as 2 or 4 cups in freezer bags. Defrost by placing the frozen block of stock in a shallow saucepan and cooking on low until the stock is completely liquid.

"Baked" Apples

Serve these lightly spiced apples as a simple dessert or a breakfast treat.

INGREDIENTS | **SERVES 6**

6 baking apples
½ cup water
1 cinnamon stick
1" knob peeled fresh ginger
1 vanilla bean

Baking with Apples

When baking or cooking, choose apples with firm flesh such as Granny Smith, Jonathan, McIntosh, Cortland, Pink Lady, Pippin, or Winesap. They will be able to hold up to low cooking times without turning to mush. Leaving the skin on adds fiber.

1. Place the apples in a simple layer on the bottom of a 4- or 6-quart slow cooker. Add the water, cinnamon stick, ginger, and vanilla bean. Cook on low for 6–8 hours or until the apples are tender and easily pierced with a fork.

2. Use a slotted spoon to remove the apples from the insert. Discard the cinnamon stick, ginger, vanilla bean, and water. Serve hot.

PER SERVING Calories: 80 | Fat: 0g | Sodium: 0mg | Carbohydrates: 20g | Fiber: 4g | Protein: 0g

Brown Bread

This version of the steamed bread is a bit fruity and spicy.

INGREDIENTS | **SERVES 20**

3 empty 16-ounce cans
Nonstick cooking spray, as needed
Bamboo skewers, to fit slow cooker
½ cup rye flour
½ cup all-purpose flour
½ cup cornmeal
1 tablespoon sugar
½ teaspoon baking powder
½ teaspoon baking soda
½ teaspoon cinnamon
½ cup sweetened dried cranberries
½ teaspoon ground ginger
1 cup fat-free buttermilk
⅓ cup molasses
Water, as needed

Slow Cooker Shapes

Most slow cookers come in round or oval shapes. Round shapes are great for soups, stews, oatmeal, chili, dips, and many layered dishes. Oval shapes are especially well suited to roasts and bulky dishes that do not fit in the narrower round slow cookers.

1. Grease the empty cans with cooking spray. Place a layer of bamboo skewers on the bottom of an oval 6-quart slow cooker. Place the cans on the skewers.

2. In a medium bowl, whisk together the flours, cornmeal, sugar, baking powder, baking soda, cinnamon, cranberries, and ginger. Set the mixture aside. In another bowl, stir together the buttermilk and molasses. Pour into the dry mixture and stir until combined.

3. Evenly divide the dough among the three cans. Cover each can with foil; stand the cans inside the slow cooker. Add water until it is halfway up the sides of the cans. Cook on low for 4–5 hours or until a toothpick inserted into the bread comes out clean.

4. Carefully remove the cans and allow them to cool for 5 minutes. Then gently tap the cans and remove the bread. Allow the bread to cool on a wire rack. Slice them into 20 slices.

PER SERVING Calories: 70 | Fat: 0.5g | Sodium: 55mg | Carbohydrates: 15g | Fiber: <1g | Protein: 1g

"Steamed" Artichokes

Choose artichokes that are all the same size so they will finish cooking at the same time.

INGREDIENTS | **SERVES 4**

4 large artichokes
1 cup water
1 lemon, cut into eighths
2 tablespoons lemon juice
1 teaspoon dried oregano

1. Place the artichokes stem-side down in an oval 4-quart slow cooker. Pour the water into the bottom of the slow cooker. Add the lemons, lemon juice, and oregano.

2. Cook on low for 6 hours or until the leaves are tender.

PER SERVING Calories: 80 | Fat: 0g | Sodium: 150mg | Carbohydrates: 19g | Fiber: 9g | Protein: 5g

Poached Figs

Use these poached figs in any recipe that calls for cooked figs or eat as-is.

INGREDIENTS | **SERVES 4**

8 ounces fresh figs
1 cup water
1 vanilla bean, split
1 tablespoon sugar

1. Put all ingredients into a 2-quart slow cooker. Cook on low for 5 hours or until the figs are cooked through and starting to split.

2. Remove the figs from the poaching liquid and serve.

PER SERVING Calories: 60 | Fat: 0g | Sodium: 0mg | Carbohydrates: 14g | Fiber: 2g | Protein: 0g

Shopping for Figs

Look for figs that are plump and soft but not squishy. The skin should not be split or oozing. Store figs in the refrigerator or in a cool dark cabinet until ready to use.

Roasted Garlic

Roasted garlic is mellow enough to eat as-is, but it is also great in any recipe that would benefit from a mild garlic flavor.

INGREDIENTS | **YIELDS 4 HEADS GARLIC**

½ tablespoon olive oil
4 heads garlic

1. Pour the oil onto the bottom of a 2-quart slow cooker. Place the garlic in a single layer on top.

2. Cook 4–6 hours on low or until the garlic is very soft and golden. To serve, simply squeeze the garlic out of the skin.

PER 1 TABLESPOON Calories: 25 | Fat: 1g | Sodium: 0mg | Carbohydrates: 4g | Fiber: 0g | Protein: 1g

Fish Stock

Use fish stock in any fish or seafood dish instead of water or chicken stock.

INGREDIENTS | **YIELDS 3 QUARTS**

3 quarts water
2 onions, quartered
Head and bones from 3 fishes, any type
2 stalks celery, chopped
2 tablespoons peppercorns
1 bunch parsley

1. Place all ingredients into a 4-quart slow cooker. Cook for 8–10 hours.

2. Remove all the solids. Refrigerate overnight. The next day, skim off any foam that has floated to the top. Use, refrigerate, or freeze the stock.

PER 1 CUP Calories: 430 | Fat: 10g | Sodium: 120mg | Carbohydrates: 37g | Fiber: 7g | Protein: 52g

CHAPTER 3

Appetizers and Snacks

Chicken Meatballs in a Hawaiian-Inspired Sauce

This is a festive appetizer for a party. Serve leftovers with short-grain rice for a quick and easy meal.

INGREDIENTS | SERVES 15

2 pounds ground chicken breast

1 teaspoon ground ginger

2 tablespoons plus ¾ cup pineapple juice, divided use

½ cup bread crumbs

1 egg

¼ cup minced onion

2 cloves garlic, grated

¼ cup soy sauce

¼ cup teriyaki sauce

¼ cup ponzu sauce

3 tablespoons lime juice

1 tablespoon cornstarch

½ tablespoon grated fresh ginger

1 small onion, thinly sliced

4 cups cubed fresh pineapple

1 jalapeño

⅓ cup brown sugar

1. Preheat the oven to 375°F. Line 2 baking sheets with parchment paper. In a large bowl, use your hands to mix the chicken, ground ginger, 2 tablespoons of pineapple juice, bread crumbs, egg, and minced onion and garlic. Form into 1" balls. Place on the baking sheets and bake for 15 minutes or until cooked through.

2. Meanwhile, in a small bowl, whisk together the remaining pineapple juice, soy sauce, teriyaki sauce, ponzu sauce, lime juice, and cornstarch. Pour into a 6-quart slow cooker.

3. Add the grated ginger, sliced onion, pineapple, jalapeño, and brown sugar to the slow cooker. Stir.

4. Add the meatballs and cook on low for 6–9 hours.

PER SERVING Calories: 170 | Fat: 5g | Sodium: 520mg | Carbohydrates: 18g | Fiber: 1g | Protein: 12g

How to Cut Up a Pineapple

Cut ½" off the bottom and top of the pineapple. Use a knife to slice off the skin and remove any "eyes." Slice the flesh from around the round core. Discard the core and cube the flesh.

Cinnamon and Sugar Peanuts

This is a festive, high-protein treat. Package the nuts in cellophane bags and give as party favors or gifts.

INGREDIENTS | **YIELDS 12 OUNCES**

12 ounces unsalted, roasted peanuts
½ tablespoon ground cinnamon
⅓ cup sugar
1 tablespoon melted butter

Place the peanuts into a 4-quart slow cooker. Add the cinnamon and sugar and drizzle with butter. Stir. Cook on low for 2–3 hours, uncovered, stirring occasionally.

PER 1 OUNCE Calories: 200 | Fat: 15g | Sodium: 0mg | Carbohydrates: 12g | Fiber: 2g | Protein: 7g

Hot and Spicy Nuts

Serve these at a cocktail party as an alternative to plain salted nuts. They are also delicious stirred into trail mix.

INGREDIENTS | **YIELDS 2½ CUPS**

2½ cups skin-on almonds or mixed nuts
1 teaspoon canola oil
½ teaspoon ground jalapeño
½ teaspoon powdered garlic
½ teaspoon ground cayenne
½ teaspoon ground chipotle
½ teaspoon ground paprika
¼ teaspoon salt

1. Place the nuts into a 2- or 4-quart slow cooker. Drizzle with oil. Stir. Add the spices, and then stir again to distribute the seasoning evenly.

2. Cook on low for 1 hour, covered; then uncover and cook on low for 15 minutes or until the nuts look dry.

PER 1 OUNCE Calories: 170 | Fat: 15g | Sodium: 45mg | Carbohydrates: 6g | Fiber: 3g | Protein: 6g

Cranberry Turkey Meatballs

Serve this easy appetizer at your next holiday party straight from the slow cooker.

INGREDIENTS | SERVES 12

28 ounces frozen, precooked turkey meatballs (about 24 meatballs)

¼ cup chili sauce

3 cups whole-berry Cranberry Sauce (page 49)

1½ tablespoons dark brown sugar

1 tablespoon ginger preserves

Simple Homemade Turkey Meatballs

In a small bowl, combine 1 pound ground turkey, ½ cup breadcrumbs, ½ teaspoon salt and pepper, ⅛ teaspoon nutmeg, and 1 minced shallot. Form into 1½" balls. Broil for 10 minutes or until cooked through.

1. Defrost the meatballs according to package instructions. Mix together the chili sauce, cranberry sauce, sugar, and preserves in a large bowl.

2. Pour half of the sauce into the bottom of a 4-quart oval slow cooker. Place the meatballs on top. Pour the remaining sauce over the meatballs. Cook on low for 4 hours or on high for 2.

PER SERVING Calories: 120 | Fat: 4g | Sodium: 250mg | Carbohydrates: 8g | Fiber: 0g | Protein: 14g

Pineapple Teriyaki Drumsticks

Serve this crowd-pleasing favorite as a hearty appetizer. Pair leftovers with steamed rice for a great lunch.

INGREDIENTS | **SERVES 12**

12 chicken drumsticks
8 ounces canned pineapple slices in juice
¼ cup low-sodium teriyaki sauce
1 teaspoon ground ginger
¼ cup hoisin sauce

1. Arrange the drumsticks in a single layer on a broiling pan. Broil for 10 minutes on high, flipping the drumsticks once halfway through the cooking time.

2. Drain the juice from the pineapple into a 4- or 6-quart oval slow cooker. Add the teriyaki sauce, ginger, and hoisin sauce. Stir to combine.

3. Cut the pineapple rings in half. Add them to the slow cooker.

4. Add the drumsticks to the slow cooker and stir to combine. Cover and cook on low for 4–6 hours.

PER SERVING Calories: 340 | Fat: 20g | Sodium: 300mg | Carbohydrates: 6g | Fiber: 0g | Protein: 31g

Almond and Dried Cherry Granola

Using the slow cooker virtually eliminates any chance of overcooking or burning the granola.

INGREDIENTS | **SERVES 24**

5 cups old-fashioned rolled oats

1 cup slivered almonds

¼ cup mild honey

¼ cup canola oil

1 teaspoon vanilla

½ cup dried tart cherries

¼ cup unsweetened flaked coconut

½ cup sunflower seeds

1. Place the oats and almonds into a 4-quart slow cooker. Drizzle with honey, oil, and vanilla. Stir the mixture to distribute the syrup evenly. Cook on high, uncovered, for 1½ hours, stirring every 15–20 minutes.

2. Add the cherries, coconut, and sunflower seeds. Reduce heat to low. Cook for 4 hours, uncovered, stirring every 20 minutes.

3. Allow the granola to cool fully, and then store it in an airtight container for up to 1 month.

PER SERVING Calories: 180 | Fat: 8g | Sodium: 0mg | Carbohydrates: 22g | Fiber: 4g | Protein: 5g

Italian Turkey Meatballs

Frozen Italian meatballs make this appetizer a snap to make. Look for them near the meat products in your grocer's freezer.

INGREDIENTS | SERVES 6

12 frozen Italian-style turkey meatballs
1 teaspoon canola oil
3 cloves garlic, minced
1 small onion, diced
1 carrot, diced
28 ounces canned crushed tomatoes
2 tablespoons tomato paste
⅛ teaspoon salt
½ teaspoon freshly ground black pepper
1 tablespoon minced basil

1. Defrost the meatballs according to package instructions. Place them into a 2- or 4-quart slow cooker.

2. Heat the oil in a nonstick pan. Sauté the garlic, onion, and carrot until the carrots and onions start to soften. Add the crushed tomatoes, tomato paste, salt, pepper, and basil. Stir. Simmer until most of the liquid has evaporated.

3. Pour the sauce over the meatballs, and stir to coat them. Cook on low up to 6 hours.

PER SERVING Calories: 170 | Fat: 8g | Sodium: 250mg | Carbohydrates: 13g | Fiber: 3g | Protein: 11g

Using Tomato Paste

Tomato paste is a thick paste made from skinned, seeded tomatoes. Its concentrated taste is perfect for slow cooking because it adds a lot of flavor without adding extra liquid. When combined with canned tomatoes, the result is a richer tasting sauce.

Mango Pork Morsels

In this recipe, the mango provides natural sweetness and a tropical flair. Plate and pierce each morsel with a toothpick.

INGREDIENTS | SERVES 10

1½ pounds lean pork loin, cubed

2 mangoes, cubed

3 cloves garlic, minced

1 jalapeño, minced

1 tablespoon salsa

¼ teaspoon salt

¼ teaspoon freshly ground black pepper

2 teaspoons ground chipotle

1 teaspoon New Mexican chili powder

½ teaspoon oregano

2 tablespoons orange juice

2 tablespoons lime juice

1. Quickly brown the pork in a nonstick skillet. Add the pork and mango to a 4-quart slow cooker.

2. In a small bowl, whisk together the garlic, jalapeño, salsa, salt, pepper, chipotle, chili powder, oregano, and the orange and lime juices. Pour over the mango and pork. Stir.

3. Cook on low for 6 hours; remove the cover and cook on high for 30 minutes. Stir before serving.

PER SERVING Calories: 120 | Fat: 2.5g | Sodium: 105mg | Carbohydrates: 9g | Fiber: 1g | Protein: 15g

How to Cut Up a Mango

Slice the mango vertically on either side of the large flat pit. Using the tip of a knife, cut vertical lines into the flesh without piercing the skin. Make horizontal lines in the flesh to form cubes. Use a spoon to scoop out the cubes. Repeat for the other side.

Light and Creamy Swedish Meatballs

All of the flavor, none of the guilt! Serve leftover meatballs over yolk-free egg noodles.

INGREDIENTS | **SERVES 20**

2 thin slices white sandwich bread

½ cup 1% milk

2 pounds 94% lean ground beef or ground chicken

2 cloves garlic, minced

1 egg

½ teaspoon allspice, divided use

¼ teaspoon nutmeg, divided use

3 cups Chicken Stock (page 17)

12 ounces fat-free evaporated milk

1 tablespoon melted butter

⅓ cup all-purpose flour

1. Preheat oven to 350°F. In a shallow saucepan, cook the bread and milk on low until the milk is absorbed, about 1 minute. Place the bread into a large bowl and add the meat, garlic, egg, ¼ teaspoon allspice, and ⅛ teaspoon nutmeg.

2. Mix until all ingredients are evenly distributed. Roll into 1" balls. Line two baking sheets with parchment paper. Place the meatballs in a single layer on the baking sheets. Bake for 15 minutes, and then drain on paper towel–lined plates.

3. Meanwhile, bring the stock, evaporated milk, butter, and remaining nutmeg and allspice to a simmer. Whisk in the flour and continue to whisk until the mixture is slightly thickened. Remove from heat.

4. Place the meatballs into a 4- or 6-quart oval slow cooker. Pour the sauce over the meatballs. Cook on low up to 6 hours. Stir gently before serving to distribute the sauce evenly.

PER SERVING Calories: 110 | Fat: 3.5g | Sodium: 125mg | Carbohydrates: 7g | Fiber: 0g | Protein: 13g

Chicken Bites

Sweet and savory flavors marry to create a simple yet satisfying appetizer.

INGREDIENTS | SERVES 16

2 pounds boneless skinless chicken breasts, cubed

1 onion, minced

2 cloves garlic, minced

½ cup chili sauce

½ cup no-sugar raspberry jam

1 tablespoon Worcestershire sauce

1 tablespoon balsamic vinegar

1. Place the chicken into a 4-quart slow cooker. In a small bowl, whisk together the onion, garlic, chili sauce, jam, Worcestershire sauce, and balsamic vinegar. Pour it over the meat.

2. Cook on low for 3 hours or until the chicken is cooked through. Stir before serving.

PER SERVING Calories: 80 | Fat: 1.5g | Sodium: 150mg | Carbohydrates: 6g | Fiber: <1g | Protein: 12g

All about Balsamic Vinegar

Balsamic vinegar has a fruity flavor that works well in sweet or savory dishes. Aged balsamic vinegar is a gourmet product that can cost more than $50. Luckily, commercial-grade balsamic is readily available and perfectly acceptable when used in marinades, salad dressings, and sauces.

Slow Cooker Snack Mix

Making a snack mix with whole-grain cereal is a breeze in the slow cooker. Unlike the oven method, there is virtually no risk of burning and little attention or hands-on time is needed.

INGREDIENTS | **SERVES 20**

2 tablespoons melted butter

1 teaspoon garlic powder

1 teaspoon onion powder

1 teaspoon paprika

1 teaspoon dried thyme

1 teaspoon dill weed

1 teaspoon chili powder

1 teaspoon Worcestershire sauce

1½ cups crispy corn cereal squares

1½ cups crispy wheat cereal squares

1½ cups crispy rice cereal squares

1 cup pretzel wheels

1 cup roasted peanuts or almonds

1. Pour the butter, spices, and Worcestershire sauce into the bottom of a 6-quart slow cooker. Stir. Add the cereal, pretzels, and nuts. Cook uncovered on low for 2–3 hours, stirring every 30 minutes.

2. Pour onto a baking sheet and allow to cool. Store in an airtight container.

PER SERVING Calories: 100 | Fat: 5g | Sodium: 150mg | Carbohydrates: 11g | Fiber: 1g | Protein: 3g

Snack Mix Variations

Mexican: Substitute 1 teaspoon each cayenne pepper, ground chipotle, hot New Mexico chili powder, and oregano for the thyme, dill weed, and Worcestershire sauce. Japanese: substitute wasabi peas for the peanuts, and 1 teaspoon each sesame seeds, soy sauce, ground ginger, and white pepper for the paprika, thyme, dill weed, and Worcestershire sauce.

Stuffed Grape Leaves

Although there are many versions of grape leaves served across the Mediterranean, these grape leaves are inspired by Greece.

INGREDIENTS | SERVES 30

16 ounces jarred grape leaves (about 60 leaves)

Cooking spray, as needed

¾ pound 94% lean ground beef, chicken, or pork

1 shallot, minced

¾ cup cooked brown or white rice

¼ cup minced dill

½ cup lemon juice, divided use

2 tablespoons minced parsley

1 tablespoon dried mint

1 tablespoon ground fennel

¼ teaspoon freshly ground black pepper

⅛ teaspoon salt

2 cups water

Easy Greek-Style Dipping Sauce

In a medium bowl, stir together 1 cup fat-free Greek yogurt and 1 teaspoon each dried oregano, mint, thyme, dill weed, and white pepper. Stir in 3 tablespoons lemon juice. Refrigerate 1 hour before serving. Refrigerate leftovers in an airtight container.

1. Prepare the grape leaves according to package instructions. Set aside.

2. Spray a nonstick skillet with cooking spray. Sauté the meat and shallot until the meat is thoroughly cooked. Drain off any excess fat. Scrape into a bowl and add the rice, dill, ¼ cup of the lemon juice, parsley, mint, fennel, pepper, and salt. Stir to incorporate all ingredients.

3. Place a leaf, stem-side up, with the top of the leaf pointing away from you on a clean work surface. Place 1 teaspoon filling in the middle of the leaf. Fold the bottom toward the middle and then fold in the sides. Roll it toward the top to seal. Repeat.

4. Place the rolled grape leaves in two or three layers in a 4-quart oval slow cooker. Pour in the water and remaining lemon juice. Cover and cook on low for 4–6 hours. Serve warm or cold.

PER SERVING Calories: 30 | Fat: 1g | Sodium: 20mg | Carbohydrates: 3g | Fiber: <1g | Protein: 3g

Balsamic Almonds

These sweet and sour almonds are a great addition to a cheese platter or appetizer plate.

INGREDIENTS | **SERVES 15**

2 cups whole almonds
½ cup dark brown sugar
½ cup balsamic vinegar
½ teaspoon kosher salt

Healthy Almonds

Botanically speaking, almonds are a seed, not a nut. They are an excellent source of vitamin E and have high levels of monoun-saturated fat, one of the two "good" fats responsible for lowering LDL cholesterol.

1. Place all ingredients into a 4-quart oval slow cooker. Cook uncovered on high for 4 hours, stirring every 15 minutes or until all the liquid has evaporated. The almonds will have a syrupy coating.

2. Line two cookie sheets with parchment paper. Pour the almonds in a single layer on the baking sheets to cool completely. Store in an airtight container for up to 1 week.

PER SERVING Calories: 150 | Fat: 10g | Sodium: 80mg | Carbohydrates: 14g | Fiber: 2g | Protein: 4g

Sticky Honey Wings

Making wings in the slow cooker is not only easy, it is a great way to keep wings warm throughout an entire party or game. Just switch the setting to warm after cooking and the wings will stay hot and sticky.

INGREDIENTS | SERVES 10

3 pounds chicken wings, tips removed
¼ cup honey
¼ cup low-sodium soy sauce
½ teaspoon freshly ground pepper
2 tablespoons chili sauce
½ teaspoon garlic powder

The World of Chili Sauce

Chili sauce is a smooth, mild red sauce. A mixture of tomato purée and spices, it is most often used as a base for other sauces. Chili-garlic sauce is a mixture of coarsely ground chilies and garlic. It is robustly flavored and used frequently in soups, stir-frys, and dipping sauces.

1. Place the wings into an oval 4-quart slow cooker.

2. In a small bowl, whisk the honey, soy sauce, pepper, chili sauce, and garlic powder. Pour over the wings. Toss to coat with sauce.

3. Cook for 6–7 hours on low. Stir before serving.

PER SERVING Calories: 340 | Fat: 22g | Sodium: 290mg | Carbohydrates: 8g | Fiber: 0g | Protein: 25g

Green Curry Wings

Green curry paste is used to make traditional Thai curries. You can find this fragrant sauce in Asian markets or in the international section of a supermarket.

INGREDIENTS | **SERVES 10**

3 pounds chicken wings, tips removed
8 ounces green curry paste
2 ounces Thai basil, minced
1 tablespoon light coconut milk
1 tablespoon minced fresh ginger
1 tablespoon minced cilantro

1. Place the wings into a 4-quart oval slow cooker.

2. In a small bowl, whisk together the curry paste, basil, coconut milk, ginger, and cilantro. Pour the sauce over the wings. Toss the wings to coat.

3. Cook on low for 6 hours. Stir prior to serving.

PER SERVING Calories: 320 | Fat: 23g | Sodium: 180mg | Carbohydrates: 1g | Fiber: 0g | Protein: 26g

CHAPTER 4

Dips and Spreads

Caramelized Onion Dip

Caramelized onions give this dip an amazing depth of flavor.

INGREDIENTS | **YIELDS 1 QUART**

⅔ cup Caramelized Onions (page 16)
8 ounces reduced-fat cream cheese
8 ounces reduced-fat or fat-free sour cream
1 tablespoon Worcestershire Sauce
¼ teaspoon white pepper
⅛ teaspoon flour

1. Place all ingredients into a 1½- to 2-quart slow cooker.

2. Heat on low for 2 hours. Whisk before serving.

PER 2 TABLESPOONS Calories: 30 | Fat: 1.5g | Sodium: 35mg | Carbohydrates: 3g | Fiber: 0g | Protein: 1g

Pineapple-Mango Chutney

Try this as a sandwich spread or as a dip.

INGREDIENTS | **SERVES 6**

3 cups cubed fresh pineapple
1½ cups cubed fresh mango
1 tablespoon grated fresh ginger
2 tablespoons minced onion
¼ cup balsamic vinegar
2 cloves garlic, minced
3 tablespoons lime juice
⅓ cup dark brown sugar
1 jalapeño, minced

1. Put all ingredients into a 2- to 4-quart slow cooker. Stir. Turn to high and cook 3 hours until soft.

2. Uncover and continue to cook on high for 1 hour.

PER SERVING Calories: 130 | Fat: 0g | Sodium: 10mg | Carbohydrates: 34g | Fiber: 2g | Protein: 1g

Black and White Bean Dip

Cannellini beans make this dip incredibly creamy.

INGREDIENTS | **SERVES 25**

1 teaspoon canola oil

1 habanero pepper, seeded and minced

1 small onion, diced

3 cloves garlic, minced

½ teaspoon hot paprika

¼ teaspoon cumin

¼ cup reduced-fat sour cream

2 tablespoons lime juice

15 ounces canned black beans, drained and rinsed

15 ounces canned cannellini beans, drained and rinsed

Paprika

Hungarian paprika comes in two aptly named varieties: sweet and hot. The spice is used to flavor and, in some cases, color dishes. Spanish paprika is also known as smoked paprika and adds a smoky, spicy note to food.

1. Heat the oil in a nonstick skillet. Sauté the habanero, onion, and garlic until soft and fragrant, about 2–3 minutes. Pour into a medium-sized bowl. Add the spices, sour cream, lime juice, and beans. Mash the mixture with a potato masher until the dip looks creamy but with some black and white beans still distinct.

2. Scrape into a 1½- to 2-quart slow cooker. Cook on low for 2 hours. Stir before serving.

PER SERVING Calories: 35 | Fat: 1g | Sodium: 120mg | Carbohydrates: 6g | Fiber: 2g | Protein: 2g

Black Bean and Corn Dip

Try this dip with whole-grain tortilla chips or pita crisps.

INGREDIENTS | **SERVES 16**

1 teaspoon canola oil

1 jalapeño, seeded and minced

1 small onion, diced

2 cloves garlic, minced

½ teaspoon ground cayenne

¼ teaspoon cumin

2 tablespoons lime juice

¼ teaspoon green hot sauce

¼ cup reduced-fat sour cream

15 ounces canned black beans, drained and rinsed

½ cup fresh or defrosted frozen corn kernels

1. Heat the oil in a nonstick skillet. Sauté the jalapeño, onion, and garlic until soft and fragrant, about 2–3 minutes. Pour into a medium-sized bowl. Add the spices, lime juice, green hot sauce, sour cream, and beans. Mash with a potato masher until most of the beans are mashed. Stir in the corn.

2. Scrape into a 1½–2 quart slow cooker. Cook on low for 2 hours. Stir before serving.

PER SERVING Calories: 35 | Fat: 1g | Sodium: 135mg | Carbohydrates: 7g | Fiber: 2g | Protein: 2g

Black Bean Facts

Black beans are also known as turtle beans. They are an excellent source of cholesterol-lowering fiber. They are also virtually fat free, making them a great addition to dips, chili, and side dishes.

Pizza Dip

Serve this low-fat dip with pita chips, crackers, a sliced baguette, soft pretzels, or garlic bread.

INGREDIENTS | **SERVES 16**

½ teaspoon canola oil

¼ cup diced onion

2 cloves garlic, minced

¼ cup quartered turkey pepperoni

½ teaspoon minced basil

2¼ ounces canned sliced black olives, drained

28 ounces canned, crushed, or coarsely ground tomatoes

Cooking with Smaller Slow Cookers

Small (1½- to 2-quart) slow cookers are great for making meals for two, side dishes, and dips. A cooker with variable settings rather than a dip-only model, where the only settings are on or off, will allow you to cook full meals for two.

1. Heat the oil in a nonstick skillet. Add the onions and garlic and sauté until the onions are soft.

2. Put the onions, garlic, pepperoni, basil, olives, and tomatoes into a 1½–2 quart slow cooker. Stir to distribute the ingredients evenly. Cook on low for 2 hours or on high for 1 hour.

PER SERVING Calories: 30 | Fat: 1g | Sodium: 135mg | Carbohydrates: 4g | Fiber: 1g | Protein: 1g

Broccoli Dip

Serve this vegetable-rich creamy dip with crisp raw vegetables and pumpernickel pretzels.

INGREDIENTS | SERVES 15

4 cups steamed broccoli florets

1 cup fresh baby spinach

1 shallot

1 jalapeño, stem and seeds removed

1 tablespoon Worcestershire sauce

½ tablespoon nonpareil capers

1 cup nonfat plain yogurt

¼ teaspoon freshly ground black pepper

2 tablespoons lemon juice

1. Place the broccoli, spinach, shallot, jalapeño, Worcestershire sauce, and capers in a food processor. Pulse until the mixture is mostly smooth. Add the yogurt, pepper, and lemon juice. Pulse until smooth.

2. Pour into a 1½- or 2-quart slow cooker. Cover and cook on low for 1 hour.

PER SERVING Calories: 20 | Fat: 0g | Sodium: 40mg | Carbohydrates: 4g | Fiber: <1g | Protein: 2g

How to Steam Vegetables

Bring about 1" of water to boil in a heavy-bottomed pot. Add the vegetables and cook until fork-tender but not soft. Drain and season.

Creamy, Low-Fat Spinach-Artichoke Dip

Try this lighter version of the classic dip at your next party. It is great with raw vegetables and pita chips.

INGREDIENTS | SERVES 15

½ teaspoon canola oil

½ cup diced onion

8 ounces frozen artichoke hearts, defrosted

3 ounces baby spinach

¼ cup diced red onion

6 ounces reduced-fat sour cream

1 tablespoon Worcestershire sauce

¼ teaspoon salt

½ teaspoon freshly ground black pepper

⅓ cup reduced-fat Italian-blend cheese

1. Heat the oil in a nonstick skillet. Sauté the onions, artichokes, spinach, and red onions until the onions are translucent and the spinach wilts. Drain any extra liquid.

2. Place into a 2-quart slow cooker. Stir in sour cream, Worcestershire sauce, salt, pepper, and cheese.

3. Cover and cook for 1 hour on low. Stir before serving.

PER SERVING Calories: 35 | Fat: 2g | Sodium: 95mg | Carbohydrates: 3g | Fiber: 1g | Protein: 2g

Cooking with Artichoke Hearts

Frozen artichoke hearts are an affordable way to use artichokes. They are fat free and ready to use. If the hearts are very large, cut them in half for easier eating.

Baba Ganoush

Serve this with pita and fresh vegetables.

INGREDIENTS	SERVES 12

1 1-pound eggplant
2 tablespoons tahini
2 tablespoons lemon juice
2 cloves garlic

Tahini Tips

Tahini is a paste made from ground sesame seeds. The most common tahini uses seeds that have been toasted before they are ground, but "raw" tahini is also available. The two can be used interchangeably in most recipes, but occasionally a recipe will specify one or the other. Look for tahini near the peanut butter, in the health food section, or with the specialty foods in most grocery stores.

1. Pierce the eggplant with a fork. Cook on high in a 4-quart slow cooker for 2 hours.

2. Allow to cool. Peel off the skin. Slice it in half and remove the seeds. Discard the skin and seeds.

3. Place the pulp in a food processor and add the remaining ingredients. Pulse until smooth.

PER SERVING | Calories: 25 | Fat: 1.5g | Sodium: 0mg | Carbohydrates: 3g | Fiber: 2g | Protein: 1g

Cranberry Sauce

Serve this sweet-tart cranberry sauce with a holiday meal; use it as a spread or pour it over ice cream.

INGREDIENTS | **SERVES 10**

12 ounces fresh cranberries
½ cup freshly squeezed orange juice
½ cup water
½ teaspoon orange zest
½ teaspoon agave nectar

Place all ingredients into a 1½- or 2-quart slow cooker. Cook on high for 2½ hours. Stir before serving.

PER SERVING Calories: 20 | Fat: 0g | Sodium: 0mg | Carbohydrates: 5g | Fiber: 2g | Protein: 0g

Slow-Cooked Salsa

This may be the easiest salsa recipe ever, but it tastes so much fresher than jarred salsa.

INGREDIENTS | **SERVES 10**

4 cups grape tomatoes, halved
1 small onion, thinly sliced
2 jalapeños, diced
⅛ teaspoon salt

1. Place all ingredients into a 2-quart slow cooker. Stir. Cook on low for 5 hours.

2. Stir and lightly smash the tomatoes before serving, if desired.

PER SERVING Calories: 20 | Fat: 0g | Sodium: 35mg | Carbohydrates: 4g | Fiber: 1g | Protein: 1g

Shrimp and Artichoke Dip

This unusual dip is delicious with sesame pretzels or pita chips.

INGREDIENTS | **SERVES 20**

8 ounces reduced-fat cream cheese

½ cup reduced-fat sour cream

½ cup diced green onion

1 tablespoon Worcestershire sauce

1½ teaspoons Chesapeake Bay seasoning

12 ounces frozen artichoke hearts, defrosted

8 ounces peeled salad shrimp

Cooking with Cream Cheese

While reduced-fat cream cheese can be successfully cooked, fat-free cream cheese separates when heated. Do not use fat-free cream cheese unless it is specifically called for. In addition, always use brick cream cheese. Whipped or spreadable cream cheese has additives to make it spread easily that separate during cooking.

1. Place the cream cheese, sour cream, green onion, Worcestershire sauce, and Chesapeake Bay seasoning in a food processor. Pulse until smooth and well blended. Add the artichoke hearts and pulse twice.

2. Scrape into a medium bowl. Add the shrimp and stir to evenly distribute.

3. Scrape into a 2-quart slow cooker. Cook on low 40 minutes. Stir before serving.

PER SERVING Calories: 50 | Fat: 3g | Sodium: 220mg | Carbohydrates: 3g | Fiber: <1g | Protein: 4g

Baltimore Crab Dip

This dip is on the table at practically every party held in Baltimore, Maryland, where blue crab is king.

INGREDIENTS | SERVES 22

1½ tablespoons Chesapeake Bay seasoning

1 teaspoon dry mustard

½ teaspoon garlic powder

8 ounces reduced-fat cream cheese, at room temperature

⅓ cup reduced-fat sour cream

1 teaspoon lemon juice

1 shallot, grated

16 ounces blue crab claw meat

1½ teaspoons Worcestershire sauce

1½ tablespoons canola oil mayonnaise

⅓ cup grated reduced-fat sharp Cheddar cheese

Homemade Chesapeake Bay Seasoning

In a small bowl, whisk together 1 tablespoon ground bay leaves, 2 teaspoons celery seed, 1¼ teaspoons dry mustard, 1 teaspoon freshly ground black pepper, ½ teaspoon garlic powder, ½ teaspoon ground nutmeg, ¼ teaspoon ground cloves, ¼ teaspoon ground ginger, ½ teaspoon paprika, ½ teaspoon ground cayenne, ⅛ teaspoon ground mace, and ⅛ teaspoon ground cardamom. Store in an airtight container up to one year.

1. In a medium bowl, thoroughly mix together the spices, cream cheese, sour cream, lemon juice, shallot, crab, Worcestershire sauce, and mayonnaise. Scrape into a 2-quart slow cooker.

2. Smooth the top of the dip and sprinkle with an even layer of cheese. Cover and cook on low for 45–60 minutes before serving.

PER SERVING Calories: 45 | Fat: 3.5g | Sodium: 200mg | Carbohydrates: 2g | Fiber: 0g | Protein: 2g

Blackberry Compote

Try this on toast or an English muffin.

INGREDIENTS | SERVES 6

2 cups blackberries
¼ cup sugar
¼ cup water

Place all ingredients into a 2-quart slow cooker. Cook on low for 3 hours, remove the lid, and cook on high for 4 hours.

PER SERVING Calories: 50 | Fat: 0g | Sodium: 0mg | Carbohydrates: 13g | Fiber: 2g | Protein: 1g

Pear Butter

Try this creamy spread on English muffins, oatmeal, or even as an ingredient in barbecue sauce.

INGREDIENTS | YIELDS 3 QUARTS

9 Bartlett pears, sliced
1 cup water or pear cider
¼ cup brown sugar
¼ cup sugar
¼ teaspoon ginger
¼ teaspoon cinnamon
¼ teaspoon mace

1. Place all ingredients in a 4-quart slow cooker. Cook on low for 10–12 hours.

2. Uncover and cook on low for an additional 10–12 hours or until thick and most of the liquid has evaporated.

3. Allow to cool completely; then pour into the food processor and purée. Pour into clean glass jars. Refrigerate.

PER 2 TABLESPOONS Calories: 15 | Fat: 0g | Sodium: 0mg | Carbohydrates: 3g | Fiber: 0g | Protein: 0g

Hummus

Serve this Middle Eastern spread with pita, vegetables, or falafel.

INGREDIENTS | **SERVES 20**

1 pound dried chickpeas

Water, as needed

3 tablespoons tahini

3 tablespoons lemon juice

3 cloves garlic

¼ teaspoon salt

Easy Snacking

Keeping hummus and fresh vegetables around makes healthy snacking easy. Cut carrots, celery, and radishes into snack-friendly sizes. Place them in a bowl with a tightly fitting lid. Fill the bowl two-thirds with water. They will keep crisp in the refrigerator up to 1 week.

1. Place the chickpeas in a 4-quart slow cooker and cover with water. Soak overnight. The next day, cook on low for 8 hours.

2. Drain, reserving the liquid. Place the chickpeas, tahini, lemon juice, garlic, and salt in a food processor. Pulse until smooth, adding the reserved liquid as needed to achieve the desired texture.

PER SERVING Calories: 40 | Fat: 1.5g | Sodium: 100mg | Carbohydrates: 6g | Fiber: 1g | Protein: 2g

Mixed Veggie Dip

Try this vegetable-rich dip with pita chips or baked potato chips.

INGREDIENTS | SERVES 20

8 ounces low-fat cream cheese, at room temperature

½ cup reduced-fat sour cream

1 teaspoon low-fat mayonnaise

½ teaspoon white pepper

½ teaspoon garlic powder

½ teaspoon onion powder

½ teaspoon Worcestershire sauce

1 carrot, minced

1 stalk celery, minced

3 tablespoons minced fresh spinach

¼ cup minced broccoli

Thoroughly mix all ingredients in a 2-quart slow cooker. Cook on low for 2 hours. Stir before serving.

PER SERVING Calories: 40 | Fat: 3g | Sodium: 45mg | Carbohydrates: 2g | Fiber: 0g | Protein: 2g

Summer Fruit Dip

Kiwi, strawberries, star fruit, banana, and citrus are all excellent dipping choices for this fruity dip, which is also delicious served cold.

INGREDIENTS | SERVES 20

½ cup raspberry purée

8 ounces reduced-fat cream cheese, at room temperature

1 tablespoon sugar

¾ cup reduced-fat sour cream

1 teaspoon vanilla

In a small bowl, whisk together all ingredients. Pour into a 2-quart slow cooker. Cook on low for 1 hour. Stir before serving.

PER SERVING Calories: 45 | Fat: 3g | Sodium: 40mg | Carbohydrates: 3g | Fiber: 0g | Protein: 2g

Sun-Dried Tomato and Pesto Dip

Tart, rich sun-dried tomatoes are the perfect partner for a fresh-tasting pesto in this creamy dip.

INGREDIENTS | **SERVES 20**

2 cloves garlic

1 tablespoon reduced-fat mayonnaise

¾ ounce fresh basil

1 teaspoon toasted pine nuts

¼ teaspoon white pepper

¼ cup julienne-cut dry (not oil-packed) sun-dried tomatoes

8 ounces reduced-fat cream cheese or Neufchâtel, at room temperature

1. Place the garlic, mayonnaise, basil, pine nuts, and pepper in a food processor. Pulse until a fairly smooth paste forms. Add the sun-dried tomatoes and pulse 4–5 times. Add the cream cheese and pulse until smooth.

2. Scrape into a 2-quart slow cooker. Cook on low for 1 hour. Stir before serving.

PER SERVING Calories: 35 | Fat: 3g | Sodium: 65mg | Carbohydrates: 1g | Fiber: 0g | Protein: 1g

How to Toast Pine Nuts

Preheat the oven to 350°F. Place the pine nuts on a cookie sheet or cake pan. Roast for 5–8 minutes in the oven. Pine nuts will be slightly browned and fragrant when fully toasted. Cool before using.

Mixed Seafood Dip

Many stores carry frozen mixes of cooked seafood like shrimp, scallops, squid, and clams. Defrost overnight in the refrigerator before using.

INGREDIENTS | SERVES 12

8 ounces reduced-fat cream cheese

½ cup reduced-fat sour cream

½ cup diced green onion

⅔ cup minced cooked mixed seafood

1 tablespoon tarragon vinegar

1 tablespoon minced parsley

1 teaspoon dried chopped onion

⅛ teaspoon celery seed

1. In a medium bowl, stir together all ingredients. Scrape into a 2-quart slow cooker. Cook on low for 1 hour or until heated through.

2. Stir before serving.

PER SERVING Calories: 70 | Fat: 4.5g | Sodium: 95mg | Carbohydrates: 2g | Fiber: 0g | Protein: 5g

Little Dipper

Slice a baguette into ⅛"-thick slices. Brush lightly with olive oil and sprinkle with dried tarragon and rosemary. Bake at 350°F for 10 minutes or until crisp.

Fig and Ginger Spread

This rich-tasting spread is great swirled into Greek yogurt or spread on a whole-wheat English muffin.

INGREDIENTS | SERVES 25

2 pounds fresh figs

2 tablespoons minced fresh ginger

2 tablespoons lime juice

½ cup water

¾ cup sugar

1. Place all ingredients in a 2-quart slow cooker. Stir. Cook on low for 2–3 hours. Remove the lid and cook an additional 2–3 hours until the mixture is thickened.

2. Pour into airtight containers and refrigerate up to 6 weeks.

PER SERVING Calories: 50 | Fat: 0g | Sodium: 0mg | Carbohydrates: 13g | Fiber: 1g | Protein: 0g

Apple and Pear Spread

Make the most of in-season apples and pears in this easy alternative to apple or pear butter.

INGREDIENTS | **YIELDS 3 QUARTS**

4 Winesap apples, cored and sliced

4 Bartlett pears, cored and sliced

1 cup water or pear cider

¼ cup brown sugar

¼ cup sugar

¼ teaspoon ginger

¼ teaspoon cinnamon

¼ teaspoon nutmeg

¼ teaspoon allspice

Do-It-Yourself Brown Sugar

Brown sugar is simply white sugar that has been mixed with molasses. Make brown sugar by combining 1 cup granulated sugar with a ¼ cup molasses. Store in an airtight container.

1. Place all ingredients into a 4-quart slow cooker. Cook on low for 10–12 hours.

2. Uncover and cook on low for an additional 10–12 hours or until thick and most of the liquid has evaporated.

3. Allow to cool completely then pour into the food processor and purée. Pour into clean glass jars. Refrigerate up to 6 weeks.

PER 2 TABLESPOONS Calories: 10 | Fat: 0g | Sodium: 0mg | Carbohydrates: 3g | Fiber: 0g | Protein: 0g

CHAPTER 5

Soups and Stews

Minestrone Soup

Minestrone is a classic Italian vegetable soup. The zucchini and cabbage are added at the end for a burst of fresh flavor.

INGREDIENTS | SERVES 8

3 cloves garlic, minced

15 ounces canned fire-roasted diced tomatoes

28 ounces canned crushed tomatoes

2 stalks celery, diced

1 medium onion, diced

3 medium carrots, diced

3 cups Roasted Vegetable Stock (page 19) or Chicken Stock (page 17)

30 ounces canned kidney beans, drained and rinsed

2 tablespoons tomato paste

2 tablespoons minced basil

2 tablespoons minced oregano

2 tablespoons minced Italian parsley

1½ cups shredded cabbage

¾ cup diced zucchini

1 teaspoon salt

½ teaspoon pepper

8 ounces small cooked pasta

Add the garlic, diced and crushed tomatoes, celery, onions, carrots, stock, beans, tomato paste, basil, and spices to a 4-quart slow cooker. Cook on low heat for 6–8 hours. Add shredded cabbage and zucchini and turn to high for the last hour. Stir in the salt, pepper, and pasta before serving.

PER SERVING Calories: 270 | Fat: 1.5g | Sodium: 900mg | Carbohydrates: 55g | Fiber: 10g | Protein: 13g

Suggested Pasta Shapes for Soup

Anchellini, small shells, hoops, alfabeto, or ditaletti are all small pasta shapes suitable for soup. For heartier soups, try bow ties or rotini. Thin rice noodles or vermicelli are better for Asian-style soups.

Mushroom Barley Soup

Using three types of mushrooms adds a lot of flavor to this soup.

INGREDIENTS | **SERVES 8**

1 ounce dried porcini mushrooms

1 cup boiling water

1½ teaspoons butter

5 ounces sliced fresh shiitake mushrooms

4 ounces sliced fresh button mushrooms

1 large onion, diced

1 clove garlic, minced

⅔ cup medium pearl barley

¼ teaspoon ground black pepper

6 cups beef broth

Hearty Vegetarian Variation

Add 1 diced carrot, 1 diced celery stalk, and 1 diced red potato with the rest of the ingredients. Use Roasted Vegetable Stock (page 19) instead of beef broth. Stir in some fresh thyme prior to serving.

1. Place the dried porcini mushrooms in a heat-safe bowl. Pour the boiling water over the mushrooms. Soak for 15 minutes.

2. Meanwhile, melt the butter in a medium skillet. Sauté the fresh mushrooms, onion, and garlic until the onions are soft.

3. Drain the porcini mushrooms and discard the water. Add all of the mushrooms, onions, garlic, barley, pepper, and the broth to a 4-quart slow cooker. Stir. Cook 6–8 hours on low.

PER SERVING Calories: 110 | Fat: 1.5g | Sodium: 590mg | Carbohydrates: 20g | Fiber: 4g | Protein: 6g

Summer Borscht

Serve this cooling soup with a dollop of sour cream, sliced cucumbers, and sliced hard-boiled eggs.

INGREDIENTS | SERVES 6

3½ cups shredded cooked beets (try using the "Roasted" Beets, page 188)

¼ cup diced onion

½ teaspoon salt

1 teaspoon sugar

¼ cup lemon juice

½ tablespoon celery seed

2 cups Chicken Stock (page 17) or Roasted Vegetable Stock (page 19)

2 cups water

1 egg (optional)

Can't Beat Beets

Beets, also known as beetroot, can be peeled, steamed, cooked, pickled, and shredded; they are good hot or cold. They are high in folate, vitamin C, potassium, and fiber. Although they have the highest sugar content of all vegetables, beets are very low in calories; one beet is only 75 calories.

1. Place the beets, onion, salt, sugar, lemon juice, celery seed, stock, and water in a 4-quart slow cooker. Cook on low for 6–8 hours or on high for 4 hours.

2. Crack the egg into a heatproof bowl. Whisk until the egg is frothy. Slowly add about ½ cup hot soup in a single stream to the egg while continually whisking. This will cook the egg. Pour the mixture back into the slow cooker. Stir and cook an additional 15 minutes. This egg step is optional but makes for a creamier soup.

3. Refrigerate the soup for 4 hours or overnight. Serve cold.

PER SERVING Calories: 80 | Fat: 1.5g | Sodium: 390mg | Carbohydrates: 15g | Fiber: 2g | Protein: 4g

Hot and Sour Soup

*Bamboo shoots, mushrooms, and vinegars can be found in the
Asian section of most well-stocked grocery stores.*

INGREDIENTS | SERVES 8

4 cups Chicken Stock (page 17) or
Roasted Vegetable Stock (page 19)

15 ounces canned straw mushrooms,
drained

7 ounces cubed extra-firm tofu

6 ounces canned bamboo shoots,
drained

3 tablespoons rice vinegar

2 tablespoons Chinese black vinegar

1 tablespoon garlic-chili sauce

3 tablespoons soy sauce

1 teaspoon freshly ground black pepper

1 teaspoon white pepper

½ teaspoon sesame oil

½ teaspoon hot chile oil

¾ cup snow peas

Place all ingredients into a 4-quart slow cooker. Stir.
Cook on low for 8 hours or on high for 3½ hours.

PER SERVING Calories: 90 | Fat: 3g | Sodium: 770mg |
Carbohydrates: 10g | Fiber: 2g | Protein: 8g

Slow Cooking with Tofu

Tofu is low in calories, a good source of
iron, and virtually fat free. It is also a good
source of protein, which makes it an attractive choice in vegetarian dishes. Extra-firm
tofu is the best choice for slow cooker recipes because the solid texture holds up well
during long cooking times.

Black Bean Soup

This is excellent served with Corn Bread (page 18).

INGREDIENTS | SERVES 8

3 slices turkey bacon

1 teaspoon canola oil

1 medium onion, diced

1 habanero pepper, seeded and minced

3 cloves garlic, minced

1 stalk celery, diced

1 carrot, diced

30 ounces canned black beans, drained and rinsed

3 cups Chicken Stock (page 17) or Spicy Smoked Turkey Stock (page 20)

Hints about Habaneros

Green habanero peppers are not ripe; when they are ready to eat, they range in color from yellow to bright red. Habanero peppers have a spicy, fruity flavor and are quite hot. If you prefer a milder dish, you can substitute an equal number of jalapeños.

1. Cook the turkey bacon in a nonstick skillet until crisp. Drain on paper towel–lined plates. Crumble the bacon into small pieces.

2. Heat the oil in a nonstick skillet. Add the onions, habanero, garlic, celery, and carrot. Sauté until the onions are soft, about 2–4 minutes.

3. Put the beans, onion mixture, and bacon crumbles into a 4-quart slow cooker. Add the broth and stir. Cook on low for 8–10 hours or on high for 4 hours.

PER SERVING Calories: 120 | Fat: 3.5g | Sodium: 730mg | Carbohydrates: 24g | Fiber: 7g | Protein: 8g

Tortilla Soup

This soup tastes even better the next day. Have it for dinner one day and lunch the next.

INGREDIENTS | SERVES 8

1 teaspoon cumin

1 teaspoon chili powder

1 teaspoon smoked paprika

⅛ teaspoon salt

25 ounces canned crushed tomatoes

14 ounces canned fire-roasted diced tomatoes

3 cups Chicken Stock (page 17) or Spicy Smoked Turkey Stock (page 19)

2 cloves garlic, minced

1 medium onion, diced

4 ounces canned diced green chiles, drained

2 habanero peppers, diced

1 cup fresh corn kernels

2 cups cubed cooked chicken or turkey breast

Tortilla strips, as desired (see below)

1. Place the spices, tomatoes, stock, garlic, onions, chiles, and peppers in a 4-quart slow cooker. Cover, and cook on low for 6 hours.

2. After 6 hours, add the corn and turkey or chicken. Cover and cook for an additional 45–60 minutes. Serve with tortilla strips.

PER SERVING Calories: 170 | Fat: 3g | Sodium: 350mg | Carbohydrates: 21g | Fiber: 4g | Protein: 17g

Put the Tortilla in Tortilla Soup

Slice 4 corn tortillas in half, then into ¼" strips. Heat ½ teaspoon canola oil in a shallow skillet. Add the tortilla strips and cook, turning once, until they are crisp and golden. Drain on paper towel–lined plates. Blot dry. Divide evenly among the bowls of soup before serving.

Greek-Style Orzo and Spinach Soup

Lemon zest adds a bright, robust flavor to this simple soup.

INGREDIENTS | **SERVES 6**

2 cloves garlic, minced

3 tablespoons lemon juice

1 teaspoon lemon zest

5 cups Chicken Stock (page 17)

1 small onion, thinly sliced

1 cup cubed cooked chicken breast

⅓ cup dried orzo

4 cups fresh baby spinach

Quick Tip: Zesting

There are many tools on the market that are for zesting citrus, but all you really need is a fine grater. Be sure to take off the outermost part of the peel, where the aromatic essential oils that hold the flavor are located. The white pith underneath is bitter and inedible.

1. Add the garlic, lemon juice, zest, stock, and onions to a 4-quart slow cooker. Cover and cook on low for 6–8 hours.

2. Stir in the chicken and cook for 30 minutes on high. Add the orzo and spinach. Stir and continue to cook on high for an additional 15 minutes. Stir before serving.

PER SERVING Calories: 150 | Fat: 3.5g | Sodium: 330mg | Carbohydrates: 16g | Fiber: 1g | Protein: 14g

Split Pea Soup

Make this soup before you go to bed and have a hot lunch ready the next day!

INGREDIENTS | SERVES 6

½ cup green split peas

½ cup yellow split peas

1 large carrot, diced

1 large parsnip, diced

1 stalk celery, diced

1 medium onion, diced

2 shallots, minced

4 ounces 98% fat-free ham steak, diced

1 teaspoon minced fresh sage

¼ teaspoon dill weed

¼ teaspoon celery seed

¼ teaspoon ground cayenne

1 teaspoon hickory liquid smoke

½ teaspoon celery flakes

½ teaspoon dried chervil

5 cups water

1. Place all ingredients into a 4-quart slow cooker. Stir. Cook on low for 12–15 hours.

2. If the soup is wetter than desired, uncover and cook on high for 30 minutes before serving.

PER SERVING Calories: 230 | Fat: 1g | Sodium: 260mg | Carbohydrates: 43g | Fiber: 2g | Protein: 16g

Using Split Peas

Carefully pick over split peas to remove any stones or stems that might be present. Rinse them off and they are ready to use. Split peas are one of the few legumes that do not need to be presoaked or cooked before slow cooking.

Posole

This rich-tasting stew just needs a sprinkling of shredded red cabbage to finish it to perfection.

INGREDIENTS | **SERVES 6**

8 large, dried New Mexican red chiles
1½ quarts Chicken Stock (page 17) or water
3 cloves garlic, minced
2 tablespoons lime juice
1 tablespoon ground cumin
1 tablespoon oregano
2 pounds boneless pork loin, cubed
¾ cup flour
1 teaspoon canola oil
1 large onion, sliced
40 ounces canned hominy

Citrus Leftovers

If you have a small amount of juice left, pour it into an ice cube tray in your freezer, one well at a time if necessary. Zest can be refrigerated up to 1 week or frozen in a freezer-safe container up to 1 month.

1. Seed the chiles, reserving the seeds. In a dry, hot frying pan, heat the chiles until warmed through and fragrant. Do not burn or brown them. Place the chiles and seeds in a medium pot with 1 quart broth or water, garlic, lime juice, cumin, and oregano. Bring to a boil and continue to boil for 20 minutes.

2. Meanwhile, in a plastic bag, toss the cubed pork with the flour to coat. Heat the oil in a large nonstick skillet and brown the meat on all sides. Add the onions and cook about 5 minutes or until the onions are soft.

3. Pour the unused stock, hominy, and the onion and pork mixture into a 4-quart slow cooker.

4. Strain the chile-stock mixture through a mesh sieve into the slow cooker insert, mashing down with a wooden spoon to press out the pulp and juice. Discard the seeds and remaining solids.

5. Cook on low for 8 hours.

PER SERVING Calories: 370 | Fat: 8g | Sodium: 480mg | Carbohydrates: 37g | Fiber: 7g | Protein: 36g

Tlalpeño Soup

Called Caldo Tlalpeño in Spanish, this Mexican soup makes a wonderful one-dish meal.
For a variation, stir in some cubed zucchini when it is time to add the chicken.

INGREDIENTS | SERVES 8

1 teaspoon canola oil

1 small onion

2 carrots, diced

2 stalks celery, diced

4 ounces canned green chiles

2 chipotle chiles in adobo, minced

15 ounces canned chickpeas, drained

1 tablespoon adobo, from the can of chipotle chiles in adobo

6 cups Chicken Stock (page 17)

3 cups diced cooked chicken

1. Heat the oil on a nonstick skillet. Sauté the onions, carrots, and celery until the onions are translucent and the carrots are slightly softened.

2. Place the sautéed vegetables, both kinds of chiles, chickpeas, adobo, and stock into a 4-quart slow cooker. Stir. Cook on low up to 9 hours.

3. About 30–40 minutes before serving, stir in the chicken, and cook on high.

PER SERVING Calories: 250 | Fat: 6g | Sodium: 1,130mg | Carbohydrates: 24g | Fiber: 4g | Protein: 24g

Beef and Vegetable Stew

Fresh herbs brighten this hearty stew that has more than twice as many vegetables as meat.

INGREDIENTS | SERVES 4

2 teaspoons canola oil

1 large onion, diced

2 parsnips, diced

2 carrots, diced

2 stalks celery, diced

3 cloves garlic, minced

2 red skin potatoes, diced

1 tablespoon minced fresh tarragon

2 tablespoons minced fresh rosemary

1 pound lean beef top round roast, cut into 1" cubes

¼ teaspoon salt

½ teaspoon freshly ground black pepper

1½ cups water

½ cup frozen peas

1 bulb fennel, diced

1 tablespoon minced parsley

1. Heat the oil in a large skillet. Sauté the onion, parsnip, carrots, celery, garlic, potatoes, tarragon, rosemary, and beef until the ingredients begin to soften and brown. Drain off any excess fat.

2. Place the mixture into a 4-quart slow cooker. Sprinkle with salt and pepper. Pour in the water. Stir. Cook for 8–9 hours on low.

3. Add the frozen peas and fennel. Cover and cook an additional ½ hour on high. Stir in the parsley before serving.

PER SERVING Calories: 340 | Fat: 7g | Sodium: 310mg | Carbohydrates: 47g | Fiber: 9g | Protein: 30g

Gumbo

Serve this Cajun classic over a little bit of rice.

INGREDIENTS | SERVES 8

2 tablespoons butter

2 tablespoons flour

1 cubanelle pepper, diced

4 cloves garlic, diced

1 onion, diced

2 carrots, diced

2 stalks celery, diced

1 quart Chicken Stock (page 17)

2 tablespoons Cajun seasoning

4 chicken andouille sausages, sliced

1½ cups diced fresh tomatoes

2 cups diced okra

1. In a nonstick skillet, melt the butter. Add the flour and stir until the flour is golden brown. Add the pepper, garlic, onions, carrots, and celery. Sauté for 1 minute.

2. Add the mixture to a 4-quart slow cooker. Add the stock, seasoning, sausage, and tomatoes. Cook on low for 8–10 hours.

3. Add the okra for the last hour of cooking. Stir prior to serving.

PER SERVING Calories: 130 | Fat: 6g | Sodium: 680mg | Carbohydrates: 14g | Fiber: 3g | Protein: 6g

Aromatic Chicken Rice Soup

This Thai-influenced soup is wonderful when you're feeling under-the-weather. It is also a great way to use up leftover chicken and that last box of rice from Chinese takeout.

INGREDIENTS | SERVES 8

2 quarts Chicken Stock (page 17)
2 carrots, diced
2 stalks celery, diced
2" knob fresh ginger, minced
½" knob galangal root, minced
2 tablespoons lime juice
1 onion, minced
4 cloves garlic, minced
⅛ teaspoon salt
½ teaspoon freshly ground pepper
½ cup minced cilantro
1½ cups cooked rice
2 cups diced cooked chicken

1. Place the Chicken Stock, carrots, celery, ginger, galangal root, lime juice, onion, garlic, salt, and pepper in a 4-quart slow cooker. Stir. Cook on low for 7–9 hours.

2. Stir in the cilantro, rice, and chicken. Cook on high for 15–30 minutes. Stir prior to serving.

PER SERVING Calories: 210 | Fat: 4.5g | Sodium: 430mg | Carbohydrates: 23g | Fiber: 2g | Protein: 19g

Pumpkin Bisque

This simple soup is a perfect first course at a holiday meal or as a light lunch.

INGREDIENTS | SERVES 4

2 cups puréed pumpkin

4 cups water

1 cup fat-free evaporated milk

¼ teaspoon ground nutmeg

2 cloves garlic, minced

1 onion, minced

1. Place all ingredients into a 4-quart slow cooker. Stir. Cook on low for 8 hours.

2. Use an immersion blender or blend the bisque in batches in a standard blender until smooth. Serve hot.

PER SERVING Calories: 110 | Fat: 0.5g | Sodium: 80mg | Carbohydrates: 21g | Fiber: 4g | Protein: 7g

Make Your Own Pumpkin Purée

Preheat the oven to 350°F. Slice a pie pumpkin or an "eating" pumpkin into wedges and remove the seeds. Place the wedges on a baking sheet and bake until the flesh is soft, about 40 minutes. Scoop out the flesh and allow it to cool before puréeing it in a blender.

Rosemary-Thyme Stew

Lots of rosemary and thyme give this surprisingly light stew a distinctive flavor.

INGREDIENTS | **SERVES 4**

1 teaspoon canola oil

1 large onion, diced

1 tablespoon flour

1 carrot, diced

2 stalks celery, diced

2 cloves garlic, minced

1 cup diced Yukon Gold potatoes

3½ tablespoons minced fresh thyme

3 tablespoons minced fresh rosemary

1 pound boneless skinless chicken breast, cut into 1" cubes

¼ teaspoon salt

½ teaspoon freshly ground black pepper

1½ cup water or Chicken Stock (page 17)

½ cup frozen or fresh corn kernels

1. Heat the oil in a large skillet. Sauté the onion, flour, carrots, celery, garlic, potatoes, thyme, rosemary, and chicken until the chicken is white on all sides. Drain off any excess fat.

2. Put sautéed ingredients into a 4-quart slow cooker. Sprinkle with salt and pepper. Pour in the water or stock. Stir. Cook for 8–9 hours on low.

3. Add the corn. Cover and cook an additional ½ hour on high. Stir before serving.

PER SERVING Calories: 260 | Fat: 6g | Sodium: 270mg | Carbohydrates: 14g | Fiber: 3g | Protein: 37g

Matzo Ball Soup

Although it is not strictly traditional, adding dill to the matzo balls adds a fresh note to this slow-cooked soup.

INGREDIENTS | SERVES 6

2 quarts Chicken Stock (page 17)

1 stalk celery, diced

2 carrots, cut into coin-sized pieces

1 parsnip, diced

1 onion, diced

1½ cups diced cooked chicken

1 cup boiling water

1 cup matzo meal

1 egg

1½ tablespoons minced dill

1. Put the Chicken Stock, celery, carrots, parsnip, and onions into a 4-quart slow cooker. Cook on low for 6–8 hours. Add the chicken 1 hour before serving.

2. About 20 minutes before serving, mix the boiling water, matzo meal, egg, and dill in a large bowl until smooth. Form into 2" balls. Drop them into the soup, cover, and cook for 15 minutes.

PER SERVING Calories: 300 | Fat: 6g | Sodium: 520mg | Carbohydrates: 39g | Fiber: 3g | Protein: 23g

Matzo Meal Facts

Matzo meal, a product similar to bread crumbs, is made from crushed matzo. While it is available year-round, it is particularly easy to find near Passover. You can make matzo meal at home by pulsing matzo (flat unleavened crackers) in a food processor until small crumbs form. It is a necessary ingredient in matzo balls and can be used as a substitute for bread crumbs in many recipes.

Pho

This Vietnamese noodle soup is easy to make in the slow cooker.
Try it instead of chicken soup during cold and flu season.

INGREDIENTS | **SERVES 6**

1 tablespoon coriander seeds
1 tablespoon whole cloves
6 star anise
1 cinnamon stick
1 tablespoon fennel seed
1 tablespoon whole cardamom
4" knob fresh ginger, sliced
1 onion, sliced
Water, as needed
3 pounds beef knuckles or oxtails
1 quart beef stock
¾ pound thinly sliced lean beef
8 ounces Vietnamese rice noodles
½ cup chopped cilantro
½ cup chopped Thai basil
2 cups mung bean sprouts

1. Quickly heat the spices, ginger, and onion in a dry nonstick skillet until the seeds start to pop. The onion and ginger should look slightly caramelized. Place them in a cheesecloth packet and tie it securely.

2. Fill a large pot with water. Bring the water to a boil and add the beef knuckles. Boil for 10 minutes. Remove from the heat and skim off the foam that rises to the surface.

3. Place the bones and the cheesecloth packet into a 6–7 quart slow cooker. Add the stock and fill the slow cooker with water, leaving 1" of headroom. Cook on low for up to 10 hours or overnight. Strain off any solids. Remove the bones and the packet.

4. Add the sliced beef and noodles. Cook for about 15 minutes or until the beef is cooked and the noodles are tender.

5. Garnish each bowl with cilantro, basil, and sprouts.

PER SERVING Calories: 270 | Fat: 3.5g | Sodium: 110mg | Carbohydrates: 41g | Fiber: 3g | Protein: 19g

Leek, Potato, and Carrot Potage

Potage is a classic French home-style soup that is perfect for a blustery winter day.

INGREDIENTS | **SERVES 6**

4 cups sliced leeks
4 russet potatoes, peeled and cubed
2 carrots, diced
5 cups water
¼ teaspoon salt
½ teaspoon white pepper

1. Place all ingredients into a 4-quart slow cooker. Cook on low for 7 hours.

2. Purée using an immersion blender or purée in batches in a blender. Serve piping hot.

PER SERVING Calories: 160 | Fat: 0g | Sodium: 130mg | Carbohydrates: 36g | Fiber: 4g | Protein: 4g

Baked Potato Soup

This soup has the flavor of a loaded or stuffed baked potato but with less fat.

INGREDIENTS | **SERVES 6**

1 onion, sliced
4 russet potatoes, peeled and cubed
5 cups water
¼ teaspoon salt
½ teaspoon white pepper
¼ cup shredded sharp Cheddar
3 tablespoons reduced-fat sour cream
2 strips turkey bacon, cooked and crumbled
⅓ cup diced green onion

1. Place the onions, potatoes, water, salt, and pepper into a 4-quart slow cooker. Cook on low for 7 hours.

2. Purée using an immersion blender or purée in batches in a blender. Stir in the cheese, sour cream, bacon crumbles, and green onion.

PER SERVING Calories: 170 | Fat: 3.5g | Sodium: 220mg | Carbohydrates: 28g | Fiber: 3g | Protein: 6g

Cioppino

This hearty and delicious seafood stew is best served with crusty sourdough bread to sop up all the juices.

INGREDIENTS | SERVES 8

1 onion, chopped

2 stalks celery, diced

6 cloves garlic, minced

28 ounces canned diced tomatoes

8 ounces clam juice

¾ cup water or Fish Stock (page 24)

6 ounces tomato paste

1 teaspoon red pepper flakes

2 tablespoons minced oregano

2 tablespoons minced Italian parsley

1 teaspoon red wine vinegar

10 ounces catfish nuggets

10 ounces peeled raw shrimp

6 ounces diced cooked clams

6 ounces lump crabmeat

¾ cup diced lobster meat

¼ cup diced green onion

1. Place the onions, celery, garlic, tomatoes, clam juice, water or stock, tomato paste, red pepper flakes, oregano, parsley, and vinegar in a 4-quart slow cooker. Stir vigorously. Cook on low for 8 hours.

2. Add the seafood and green onions and cook on high for 30 minutes. Stir prior to serving.

PER SERVING Calories: 210 | Fat: 5g | Sodium: 510mg | Carbohydrates: 13g | Fiber: 3g | Protein: 30g

Save Your Shells

Save your shrimp shells to make shrimp stock. Simply follow the recipe for Chicken Stock (page 17) and use the shells instead of chicken bones. Add a couple of extra pieces of celery, onion, and carrot for extra flavor. Use in seafood dishes instead of fish or chicken stock.

Bouillabaisse

With one bite, this slightly simplified version of the Provençal fish stew will convert anyone who is skeptical about cooking seafood in the slow cooker into a believer.

INGREDIENTS | SERVES 8

1 bulb fennel, sliced

2 leeks, sliced

2 carrots, cut into coins

2 shallots, minced

5 cloves garlic, minced

2 tablespoons minced basil

1 tablespoon orange zest

1 tablespoon lemon zest

1 bay leaf

14 ounces canned diced tomatoes

2 quarts water or Fish Stock (page 24)

1 pound cubed hake or catfish

8 ounces medium peeled shrimp

1 pound mussels

1. Place the vegetables, garlic, basil, zests, bay leaf, tomato, and water or stock into a 6-quart slow cooker. Stir. Cook on low for 8 hours.

2. Add the seafood. Cook for 20 minutes on high. Stir prior to serving. Discard any mussels that do not open.

PER SERVING Calories: 260 | Fat: 8g | Sodium: 280mg | Carbohydrates: 23g | Fiber: 3g | Protein: 27g

French Onion Soup

Traditionally the soup is topped with loads of cheese and bread, but in this slimmed-down version, the cheesy bread is served on the side.

INGREDIENTS | SERVES 8

4 large onions, thinly sliced
½ tablespoon butter
½ tablespoon olive oil
½ teaspoon sugar
3 tablespoons flour
2 quarts beef stock or Chicken Stock (page 17)

Place the onions, butter, oil, sugar, and flour into a 4-quart slow cooker. Cook on high for 40 minutes. Add the stock and reduce to low. Cook for 8 hours.

PER SERVING Calories: 140 | Fat: 4.5g | Sodium: 350mg | Carbohydrates: 19g | Fiber: 1g | Protein: 7g

Cheese Toast

Place 4 thin slices of Italian bread on a baking sheet. Sprinkle each with a teaspoon of shredded reduced-fat Italian mixed cheese or Swiss cheese. Bake for 10 minutes at 350°F.

Curried Cauliflower Soup

Orange cauliflower is an excellent variety to use in this recipe. It has 25 percent more vitamin A than white cauliflower and lends an attractive color to the soup.

INGREDIENTS | SERVES 4

1 pound cauliflower florets

2½ cups water

1 onion, minced

2 cloves garlic, minced

3 teaspoons curry powder

¼ teaspoon cumin

1. Place all ingredients into a 4-quart slow cooker. Stir. Cook on low for 8 hours.

2. Use an immersion blender or blend the soup in batches in a standard blender until smooth.

PER SERVING Calories: 60 | Fat: 0g | Sodium: 40mg | Carbohydrates: 11g | Fiber: 4g | Protein: 4g

Curry Powder Power

Curry powder is a mixture of spices commonly used in South Asian cooking. While it does not correlate directly to any particular kind of curry, it is popular in Europe and North America to add an Indian flare to dishes. It can contain any number of spices, but nearly always includes turmeric, which gives it its distinctive yellow color.

Chili

Fiery Chicken Chili

For the hot and spicy lover! Serve with Corn Bread (page 18).

INGREDIENTS | SERVES 8

1 pound ground chicken

3 cloves garlic, chopped

3 chipotle chiles in adobo

15 ounces canned dark red kidney beans, drained and rinsed

15 ounces canned black beans, drained and rinsed

1 teaspoon Worcestershire sauce

30 ounces canned diced tomatoes

4 ounces canned diced green chiles

1 teaspoon ground cayenne

1 teaspoon ground chipotle

1 onion, chopped

1 tablespoon habanero hot sauce

1 teaspoon paprika

1 teaspoon hot chili powder

1 teaspoon liquid smoke

1. Quickly sauté the ground chicken in a nonstick skillet until just cooked through. Drain all fat.

2. Place all ingredients in a 4-quart slow cooker. Stir. Cook on low for 8–10 hours.

PER SERVING Calories: 210 | Fat: 5g | Sodium: 550mg | Carbohydrates: 30g | Fiber: 11g | Protein: 17g |

What Is Liquid Smoke?

Liquid smoke is made by condensing smoke in water to form a fluid. It is found in a variety of flavors including hickory and mesquite and can be used to add the flavor of being slow cooked over a flame without actually having to grill.

Smoky Chipotle Pork Chili

Chipotle peppers add a smoky, spicy flavor to this chili.

INGREDIENTS | SERVES 8

1 pound ground pork

30 ounces canned fire-roasted diced tomatoes

3 chipotle chiles in adobo, chopped

1 teaspoon liquid smoke

1 teaspoon chili powder

1 teaspoon ground chipotle

1 teaspoon hot paprika

1 teaspoon smoked paprika

30 ounces canned chili beans, drained and rinsed

1 medium onion, diced

3 cloves garlic, minced

1. Quickly sauté the pork in a nonstick skillet until just cooked through. Drain off any fat.

2. Place all ingredients in a 4-quart slow cooker. Stir. Cook on low for 8–10 hours.

PER SERVING Calories: 270 | Fat: 13g | Sodium: 580mg | Carbohydrates: 25g | Fiber: 9g | Protein: 17g |

What Are Chipotle Chiles in Adobo?

Chipotle peppers are smoke-dried jalapeños. They are then canned in a spiced onion, garlic, and tomato sauce. You can find them in the Mexican or ethnic foods section of most grocery stores.

Secret Ingredient Beef Chili

The mango melts into the chili and adds a fruity depth of flavor.

INGREDIENTS | SERVES 8

1 pound 94% lean ground beef

30 ounces canned diced tomatoes

¼ cup cubed mango

1 teaspoon liquid smoke

1 teaspoon chili powder

1 teaspoon ground jalapeño

1 teaspoon hot chili powder

1 teaspoon smoked paprika

30 ounces canned kidney beans, drained and rinsed

1 medium onion, diced

3 cloves garlic, minced

1 teaspoon cumin

1. Quickly sauté the beef in a nonstick skillet until no longer pink. Drain off all fat and discard it.

2. Place the beef and all the remaining ingredients in a 4-quart slow cooker. Stir. Cook on low for 8–10 hours.

PER SERVING Calories: 200 | Fat: 3.5g | Sodium: 450mg | Carbohydrates: 25g | Fiber: 9g | Protein: 19g |

Why Use Canned Beans?

Canned beans are ready to eat directly out of the package, making them an excellent time saver. Dried beans need to be soaked or cooked before using. Properly cooked dried beans can be substituted for an equal amount of canned, but resist the temptation to use uncooked dried beans unless explicitly directed to in the recipe. They may not rehydrate properly.

Acorn Squash Chili

Acorn squash keeps its shape in this chili, giving it a chunky texture.

INGREDIENTS | SERVES 8

2 cups cubed acorn squash

30 ounces canned petite diced tomatoes

2 stalks celery, diced

1 medium onion, diced

3 cloves garlic, minced

2 carrots, diced

1 teaspoon mesquite liquid smoke

2 teaspoons hot sauce

1 teaspoon chili powder

1 teaspoon paprika

1 teaspoon oregano

1 teaspoon smoked paprika

15 ounces canned kidney beans, drained and rinsed

15 ounces canned cannellini beans, drained and rinsed

1 cup fresh corn kernels

1. Place all of the ingredients except the corn in a 4-quart slow cooker. Cook for 8 hours on low.

2. Add the corn and stir. Cover and continue to cook on low for ½ hour. Stir before serving.

PER SERVING Calories: 170 | Fat: 0.5g | Sodium: 390mg | Carbohydrates: 35g | Fiber: 10g | Protein: 7g |

Cayenne versus Chili Powder

Contrary to popular belief, ground cayenne pepper and chili powder are not interchangeable. Ground cayenne is made from a dried cayenne pepper. Chili powder is mixture of several different varieties of chiles.

Three Bean Chili

This meatless chili is quite hearty; even the most dedicated meat lover will love it!

INGREDIENTS | SERVES 8

1 teaspoon minced fresh jalapeño

30 ounces canned diced tomatoes

2 stalks celery, diced

1 medium onion, diced

3 cloves garlic, minced

2 carrots, diced

1 teaspoon ground cayenne

1 teaspoon chili powder

1 teaspoon paprika

1 teaspoon cumin

2 teaspoons jalapeño hot sauce

15 ounces canned black beans, drained and rinsed

15 ounces canned kidney beans, drained and rinsed

15 ounces canned cannellini beans, drained and rinsed

1 cup fresh corn kernels

1. Place all of the ingredients except the corn into a 4-quart slow cooker. Cook for 8 hours on low.

2. Add the corn and stir. Cover and continue to cook on low for ½ hour. Stir before serving.

PER SERVING Calories: 180 | Fat: 1.5g | Sodium: 630mg | Carbohydrates: 39g | Fiber: 11g | Protein: 9g |

Chili Pairings

Try chili topped with low-fat sour cream, diced avocado, diced onions, sharp Cheddar, or diced green onions. Serve over rice or crumbled tortilla chips. Stir leftovers into cooked whole-wheat pasta and sprinkle with cheese for an easy chili mac-n-cheese.

Lean Green Chili

Green chili gets its name from tomatillos and lots of green chiles.

INGREDIENTS | SERVES 8

30 ounces canned cannellini beans, drained and rinsed

1 teaspoon cumin

1 teaspoon ground jalapeño

1 jalapeño, minced

2 cloves garlic, minced

4 ounces canned green chiles, drained

28 ounces canned tomatillos, drained

1 medium onion, diced

1 tablespoon lime juice

1 teaspoon celery flakes

1 stalk celery, diced

2 cups diced cooked chicken breast

Place all of the ingredients except the chicken in a 4-quart slow cooker. Cook on low for 8 hours. Stir in the chicken, put the lid back on, and cook for an additional hour on low. Stir before serving.

PER SERVING Calories: 190 | Fat: 3g | Sodium: 320mg | Carbohydrates: 25g | Fiber: 7g | Protein: 17g |

Time-Saving Tip

Cube leftover cooked chicken or turkey breast and freeze in clearly marked 1- or 2-cup packages. Defrost overnight in the refrigerator before using. Cooked poultry should be added to a recipe during the last hour of cooking.

Turkey-Tomatillo Chili

This is a great way to use up leftover turkey from Thanksgiving!

INGREDIENTS | **SERVES 8**

2 cups cubed tomatillos

1 green bell pepper, diced

1 onion, diced

1 teaspoon ground cayenne

1 teaspoon cumin

1 teaspoon paprika

1 teaspoon chili powder

30 ounces canned chili beans, drained and rinsed

2 cups cubed cooked turkey breast

Place all ingredients except the turkey in a 4-quart slow cooker. Stir to mix the ingredients. Cook on low for 8 hours, and then stir in the turkey. Cook for an additional 30–60 minutes on high.

PER SERVING Calories: 170 | Fat: 2g | Sodium: 390mg | Carbohydrates: 22g | Fiber: 9g | Protein: 17g |

Tomatillo Tidbits

Tomatillos, like tomatoes, are a part of the nightshade family of vegetables. They look like small tomatoes covered in a papery husk. The husk should be removed before eating. Look for tomatillos that are unblemished, slightly heavy for their size, and solid to the touch. They are most commonly green but can also be purple or yellow.

Cincinnati Chili

This unusual regional favorite has a spicy sweet flavor that is wonderfully addictive! Serve over cooked spaghetti with any combination of the following toppings: kidney beans, diced raw onion, and shredded cheddar.

INGREDIENTS | SERVES 8

1 pound 93% lean ground beef

15 ounces crushed tomato in juice

2 cloves garlic, minced

1 onion, diced

1 teaspoon cumin

1 teaspoon cocoa

2 teaspoons chili powder

½ teaspoon cloves

1 tablespoon apple cider vinegar

1 teaspoon allspice

½ teaspoon ground cayenne

1 teaspoon cinnamon

1 tablespoon Worcestershire sauce

¼ teaspoon salt

1. In a nonstick skillet, quickly sauté the beef until it is no longer pink. Drain all fat and discard it.

2. Place all ingredients—including the beef—in a 4-quart slow cooker. Stir. Cook on low for 8–10 hours.

PER SERVING Calories: 110 | Fat: 3.5g | Sodium: 210mg | Carbohydrates: 7g | Fiber: 2g | Protein: 14g |

Sauté the Meat When Making Chili

Even though it is not aesthetically necessary to brown the meat when making chili, sautéing meats before adding it to the slow cooker allows you to drain off any extra fat. Not only is it healthier to cook with less fat, your chili will be unappetizingly greasy if there is too much fat present in the meat during cooking.

Spicy Sausage Chili

You can use hot or mild reduced-fat bulk sausage in this recipe.

INGREDIENTS | SERVES 8

1½ pounds spicy chicken sausage

2 teaspoons ground cayenne

1 tablespoon ground chipotle

1 teaspoon hot paprika

1 teaspoon hot chili powder

15 ounces canned cannellini beans, drained and rinsed

15 ounces canned tomatoes with green chiles

15 ounces canned hominy

1 teaspoon cumin

1. Brown the sausage in a nonstick skillet. Drain off all fat.

2. Add the sausage and remaining ingredients to a 4-quart slow cooker and stir to combine and break up the hominy as needed. Cook on low for 8–10 hours.

PER SERVING Calories: 270 | Fat: 15g | Sodium: 1,240mg | Carbohydrates: 18g | Fiber: 4g | Protein: 14g

Mushroom Chili

Meaty Portobello mushrooms make this vegan chili very satisfying.

INGREDIENTS | SERVES 4

3 Portobello mushrooms, cubed

15 ounces canned black beans, drained and rinsed

1 onion, diced

3 cloves garlic, sliced

2½ cups diced fresh tomatoes

1 chipotle pepper in adobo, minced

½ teaspoon jalapeño hot sauce

1 teaspoon cumin

½ teaspoon ground cayenne

½ teaspoon freshly ground black pepper

¼ teaspoon salt

Place all ingredients into a 4-quart slow cooker. Stir. Cook on low for 8 hours.

PER SERVING Calories: 120 | Fat: 1.5g | Sodium: 740mg | Carbohydrates: 29g | Fiber: 9g | Protein: 8g

California Chili

This chili was inspired by Gilroy, California, a town that is world-renowned for its garlic crop and annual garlic festival.

INGREDIENTS | SERVES 6

15 ounces hominy

15 ounces fire-roasted tomatoes with garlic

½ cup canned cannellini beans, drained and rinsed

1 teaspoon cumin

1 teaspoon ground jalapeño

2 Anaheim chiles, diced

6 cloves garlic, thinly sliced

1 medium onion, diced

1 stalk celery, diced

1 tablespoon lime juice

1 teaspoon chipotle chile powder

1 teaspoon California chile powder

2 cups diced cooked chicken breast

1. Place all of the ingredients except the chicken in a 4-quart slow cooker. Cook on low for 8 hours.

2. Stir in the chicken, cover the cooker again, and cook for an additional hour on low. Stir before serving.

PER SERVING Calories: 200 | Fat: 2.5g | Sodium: 570mg | Carbohydrates: 25g | Fiber: 5g | Protein: 18g

No Bean Chili

For a variation, try this with lean beef sirloin instead of pork.

INGREDIENTS | SERVES 6

1 tablespoon canola oil

1 pound boneless pork tenderloin, cubed

1 large onion, diced

3 poblano chiles, diced

2 cloves garlic, minced

1 teaspoon cumin

1 teaspoon dried oregano

1 cup Chicken Stock (page 17)

15 ounces canned crushed tomatoes

2 teaspoons ground cayenne pepper

1. In a large nonstick skillet, heat the oil. Add the pork, onion, chiles, and garlic. Sauté until the pork is no long visibly pink on any side. Drain off any fats or oils and discard them.

2. Pour the pork mixture into a 4-quart slow cooker. Add the remaining ingredients. Stir.

3. Cook on low for 8–9 hours.

PER SERVING Calories: 190 | Fat: 7g | Sodium: 190mg | Carbohydrates: 14g | Fiber: 4g | Protein: 20g

Using Herbs

As a general rule, 1 tablespoon minced fresh herbs equals 1 teaspoon dried herbs. Fresh herbs can be frozen for future use. Discard dried herbs after 1 year.

Summer Chili

This chili is full of summer vegetables. It is also great as a vegetarian chili, simply omit the chicken.

INGREDIENTS | **SERVES 8**

½ pound ground chicken

1 bulb fennel, diced

4 radishes, diced

2 stalks celery, diced, including leaves

2 carrots, cut into coin-sized pieces

1 medium onion, diced

1 shallot, diced

4 cloves garlic, sliced

1 habanero pepper, diced

15 ounces canned cannellini beans, drained and rinsed

12 ounces tomato paste

½ teaspoon dried oregano

½ teaspoon black pepper

½ teaspoon crushed rosemary

½ teaspoon cayenne

½ teaspoon ground chipotle

1 teaspoon chili powder

1 teaspoon tarragon

¼ teaspoon cumin

¼ teaspoon celery seed

2 zucchini, cubed

10 Campari tomatoes, quartered

1 cup corn kernels

1. Sauté the meat in a nonstick pan until just browned. Add to a 4-quart slow cooker along with the fennel, radishes, celery, carrots, onion, shallot, garlic, habanero, beans, tomato paste, and all spices. Stir.

2. Cook on low for 6–7 hours; then stir in the zucchini, tomatoes, and corn. Cook for an additional 30 minutes on high. Stir before serving.

PER SERVING Calories: 200 | Fat: 3.5g | Sodium: 520mg | Carbohydrates: 35g | Fiber: 9g | Protein: 12g

Super-Mild Chili

This is a chili for those people who like the idea of chili but who are not fond of spicy food.

INGREDIENTS | SERVES 6

1 pound ground turkey

30 ounces canned cannellini beans, drained and rinsed

28 ounces crushed tomatoes

1 teaspoon oregano

½ teaspoon cumin

1 teaspoon mild chili powder

1 bell pepper, diced

1 Vidalia onion, diced

2 cloves garlic, minced

1. Brown the turkey in a nonstick skillet. Drain if needed.

2. Add the turkey and all of the remaining ingredients to a 4-quart slow cooker. Stir. Cook on low for 7–8 hours. Stir before serving.

PER SERVING Calories: 280 | Fat: 7g | Sodium: 550mg | Carbohydrates: 34g | Fiber: 9g | Protein: 21g

Texas Firehouse Chili

This no-bean chili is similar to dishes entered into firehouse chili cook-offs all over Texas.

INGREDIENTS | SERVES 4

1 pound cubed lean beef

2 tablespoons onion powder

1 tablespoon garlic powder

2 tablespoons Mexican-style chili powder

1 tablespoon paprika

½ teaspoon oregano

½ teaspoon freshly ground black pepper

½ teaspoon white pepper

½ teaspoon cayenne pepper

½ teaspoon chipotle pepper

8 ounces tomato sauce

1. Quickly brown the beef in a nonstick skillet. Drain off any excess grease.

2. Add the meat and all of the remaining ingredients to a 4-quart slow cooker. Cook on low up to 10 hours.

PER SERVING Calories: 260 | Fat: 12g | Sodium: 430mg | Carbohydrates: 12g | Fiber: 3g | Protein: 25g

Filipino-Influenced Pork Chili

*This chili, inspired by popular Filipino condiments and flavors,
is a wonderful change from American-style chili.*

INGREDIENTS | **SERVES 8**

1 pound pork loin, cubed

1½ cups crushed tomatoes

⅓ cup banana sauce

2 tablespoons lime juice

2 tablespoons cane vinegar

1 teaspoon ginger juice

1 teaspoon chili powder

½ teaspoon freshly ground black pepper

2 jarred pimentos, minced

1 onion, minced

3 unripe plantains, diced

2 tomatoes, cubed

1 large sweet potato, cubed

1. Sauté the cubed pork in a dry skillet for 5 minutes. Drain off any fat.

2. Add the pork and remaining ingredients to a 4-quart slow cooker. Stir. Cook on low for 8 hours. Stir before serving.

PER SERVING Calories: 210 | Fat: 2.5g | Sodium: 70mg | Carbohydrates: 36g | Fiber: 4g | Protein: 14g

All about Banana Sauce

Banana sauce, also known as banana ketchup, is a popular condiment in the Philippines. Despite its similar appearance to tomato ketchup, it contains a mixture of bananas, sugar, vinegar, and spices rather than tomatoes. Banana sauce is found in Filipino-style spaghetti sauce and used on hot dogs, burgers, omelets, French fries, and fish.

Sauces

Strawberry-Rhubarb Compote

Try this over Greek yogurt or pancakes.

INGREDIENTS | **YIELDS 1½ CUPS**

1 pound strawberries, diced
½ pound rhubarb, diced
2 tablespoons lemon juice
1 tablespoon lemon zest

Rhubarb Facts

The leaves of the rhubarb plant are toxic, but the stalks are perfectly edible. Despite being a tart vegetable, rhubarb is most often served in sweet dishes where its tartness contrasts with a sweeter ingredient like strawberries.

1. Place all ingredients into a 3½- to 4-quart slow cooker.

2. Cook for 2 hours on low.

3. Lightly mash with a potato masher.

4. Cook on high, uncovered, for 1 additional hour.

PER 2 TABLESPOONS Calories: 15 | Fat: 0g | Sodium: 0mg | Carbohydrates: 4g | Fiber: 1g | Protein: 0g

Homemade Barbecue Sauce

Try this spicy Georgia barbecue–inspired sauce drizzled over pork or beef sandwiches, meatballs, or in pulled pork.

INGREDIENTS | **SERVES 80**

12 ounces canned tomato paste
2 cups distilled white vinegar
2 tablespoons dark brown sugar
1½ tablespoons mustard powder
1 tablespoon ground black pepper
1½ tablespoons ground cayenne pepper
1 teaspoon salt
1 tablespoon unsalted butter

Place all ingredients into a 1½- or 2-quart slow cooker. Whisk to combine. Cook on low for 2–3 hours. Whisk smooth. Refrigerate any leftover sauce in an airtight container for up to 3 weeks.

PER SERVING Calories: 5 | Fat: 0g | Sodium: 65mg | Carbohydrates: 1g | Fiber: 0g | Protein: 0g

Puttanesca Sauce

Don't be discouraged by the anchovies; they simply melt away and add a complex flavor to this spicy, salty, garlicky sauce.

INGREDIENTS | SERVES 6

4 anchovies in oil

1 tablespoon olive oil

4 cloves garlic, minced

1 onion, diced

1 cup sliced black olives

28 ounces crushed tomatoes

15 ounces diced tomatoes

1 tablespoon crushed red pepper

2 tablespoons drained nonpareil-sized capers

What Is Sautéing?

Sautéing is a method of cooking that uses a small amount of fat to cook food in a shallow pan over medium-high heat. The goal is to brown the food while preserving its color, moisture, and flavor.

1. Pat the anchovies with a paper towel to remove any excess oil. Heat the olive oil in a large, nonstick skillet and add the anchovies, garlic, and onion. Sauté until the anchovies mostly disappear into the onions, and garlic and the onions are soft.

2. Place the onions, anchovies, and garlic into a 4-quart slow cooker. Add the remaining ingredients. Stir to distribute the ingredients evenly. Cook on low for 10–12 hours. If the sauce looks very wet at the end of the cooking time, remove the lid and cook on high for 15–30 minutes before serving.

PER SERVING Calories: 90 | Fat: 3g | Sodium: 580mg | Carbohydrates: 16g | Fiber: 5g | Protein: 4g

Shrimp Fra Diavolo

Serve this spicy sauce over hot pasta.

INGREDIENTS | SERVES 4

1 teaspoon olive oil

1 medium onion, diced

3 cloves garlic, minced

1 teaspoon red pepper flakes

15 ounces canned diced fire-roasted tomatoes

1 tablespoon minced Italian parsley

½ teaspoon freshly ground black pepper

¾ pound medium shrimp, shelled

Slow Cooking with Shrimp

When slow cooking with shrimp, resist the temptation to put the shrimp in at the beginning of the recipe. While it takes longer to overcook foods in the slow cooker, delicate shrimp can go from tender to rubbery very quickly. For most recipes, 20 minutes on high is sufficient cooking time for shrimp.

1. Heat the oil in a nonstick skillet. Sauté the onion, garlic, and red pepper flakes until the onion is soft and translucent.

2. Add the onion mixture, tomatoes, parsley, and black pepper to a 4-quart slow cooker. Stir. Cook on low for 2–3 hours.

3. Add the shrimp. Stir and cover and cook on high for 15 minutes or until the shrimp is fully cooked.

PER SERVING Calories: 140 | Fat: 2.5g | Sodium: 170mg | Carbohydrates: 11g | Fiber: 3g | Protein: 19g

Rosemary-Mushroom Sauce

Try this sauce with egg noodles. Add 8 ounces of dried egg noodles to the slow cooker at the end of the cooking time and cook on high for 15 minutes or until the noodles are tender.

INGREDIENTS | SERVES 4

1 teaspoon butter
1 large onion, thinly sliced
8 ounces sliced mushrooms
1 tablespoon crushed rosemary
3 cups Chicken Stock (page 17)

Save Time!

Buy sliced mushrooms. Most stores carry several varieties in the produce section. Crimini and button are popular small mushrooms. Portobello mushrooms are large and meaty enough to use as a meat substitute.

1. Melt the butter in a nonstick skillet. Add the onions and mushrooms and sauté until the onions are soft, about 5 minutes.

2. Place the onions and mushrooms into a 4-quart slow cooker. Add the rosemary and stock. Stir. Cook on low for 6–8 hours or on high for 3.

PER SERVING Calories: 100 | Fat: 3.5g | Sodium: 260mg | Carbohydrates: 13g | Fiber: 2g | Protein: 7g

Jalapeño-Tomatillo Sauce

Serve this sauce over rice or in burritos or tacos.

INGREDIENTS | SERVES 4

1 teaspoon canola oil
2 cloves garlic, minced
1 onion, sliced
7 tomatillos, large dice
2 jalapeños, minced
½ cup water

1. Heat the oil in a nonstick pan. Sauté the garlic, onion, tomatillos, and jalapeños until softened.

2. Place the mixture into a 4-quart slow cooker. Add the water and stir. Cook on low for 8 hours.

PER SERVING Calories: 50 | Fat: 2g | Sodium: 0mg | Carbohydrates: 8g | Fiber: 2g | Protein: 1g

Fruity Balsamic Barbecue Sauce

Use this sauce in pulled pork, as a dipping sauce, over chicken or burgers, or even as a marinade.

INGREDIENTS | **SERVES 20**

¼ cup balsamic vinegar

2½ cups cubed mango

2 chipotle peppers in adobo, puréed

1 teaspoon dark brown sugar

1. Place all ingredients into a 2-quart slow cooker. Stir. Cook on low for 6–8 hours.

2. Mash the sauce with a potato masher. Store in an airtight container for up to 2 weeks in the refrigerator.

PER SERVING Calories: 20 | Fat: 0g | Sodium: 40mg | Carbohydrates: 5g | Fiber: 0g | Protein: 0g

Italian Tomato Sauce with Turkey Meatballs

Using roasted garlic eliminates the need for sautéing, making this recipe a snap to put together.

INGREDIENTS | **SERVES 4**

12 frozen turkey meatballs

1½ tablespoons minced basil

1 medium onion, minced

1 head roasted garlic (about 2 tablespoons), peels removed

28 ounces fire-roasted tomatoes

1 teaspoon crushed red pepper flakes

Defrost the meatballs according to package instructions. Place in a 4-quart slow cooker with the remaining ingredients. Stir. Cook on low for 3–6 hours. Stir before serving.

PER SERVING Calories: 230 | Fat: 5g | Sodium: 550mg | Carbohydrates: 24g | Fiber: 5g | Protein: 20g

Peach Sauce

Try this naturally sweet sauce over yogurt, ice cream, pancakes, or waffles.

INGREDIENTS | SERVES 6

2 cups sliced peaches

½ teaspoon grated fresh ginger

2 tablespoons water

¼ teaspoon cornstarch (if necessary for thickening)

Place all ingredients into a 2-quart slow cooker and cook on low for 4 hours. If the sauce is very thin, stir in the cornstarch prior to serving. You could also substitute 2 tablespoons triple sec for the water if desired.

PER SERVING Calories: 20 | Fat: 0g | Sodium: 0mg | Carbohydrates: 5g | Fiber: <1g | Protein: 1g

Grating Ginger

When grating ginger, the stringy fibers should not end up in the finished dish. At the very least, use the finest part of a box grater. A fine zesting grater works well. The best tool is the ceramic ginger grater. Look for it in specialty stores.

Chicken Ragu

Serve this over linguine with a sprinkle of Parmesan.

INGREDIENTS | SERVES 6

1 pound boneless skinless chicken breasts, finely chopped

3 shallots, finely minced

4 cups Marinara Sauce (page 189)

2 teaspoons crushed rosemary

2 cloves garlic, minced

½ teaspoon freshly ground pepper

½ teaspoon oregano

Place all of the ingredients into a 4-quart slow cooker. Stir. Cook on low for 4–6 hours. Stir before serving.

PER SERVING Calories: 210 | Fat: 2.5g | Sodium: 70mg | Carbohydrates: 22g | Fiber: <1g | Protein: 26g

Lemon Dill Sauce

Serve this sauce over salmon, asparagus, potatoes, or chicken.

INGREDIENTS | SERVES 4

2 cups Chicken Stock (page 17)
½ cup lemon juice
½ cup chopped fresh dill
¼ teaspoon white pepper

Place all ingredients into a 2- or 4-quart slow cooker. Cook on high, uncovered, for 3 hours or until the sauce reduces by one-third.

PER SERVING Calories: 50 | Fat: 1.5g | Sodium: 170mg | Carbohydrates: 7g | Fiber: 0g | Protein: 3g

A Peek at Peppercorns

Black peppercorns are the mature fruit of the black pepper plant, which grows in tropical areas. Green peppercorns are the immature fruit of the pepper plant. White peppercorns are mature black peppercorns with the black husks removed. Pink peppercorns are the dried berries of the Brazilian pepper.

Raspberry Coulis

A coulis is a thick sauce made from puréed fruits or vegetables. In this recipe, the slow cooking eliminates the need for puréeing because the fruit cooks down enough that straining is unnecessary.

INGREDIENTS | SERVES 8

12 ounces fresh or frozen raspberries
1 teaspoon balsamic vinegar
2 tablespoons sugar

Place all ingredients into a 2-quart slow cooker. Mash gently with a potato masher. Cook on low for 4 hours uncovered. Stir before serving.

PER SERVING Calories: 35 | Fat: 0g | Sodium: 0mg | Carbohydrates: 8g | Fiber: 3g | Protein: 1g

Taste, Taste, Taste

When using fresh berries, it is important to taste them prior to sweetening. One batch of berries might be tart while the next might be very sweet. Reduce or eliminate extra sugar if using very ripe, sweet berries.

Artichoke Sauce

Slow cooking artichokes gives them a velvety texture.

INGREDIENTS | **SERVES 4**

1 teaspoon olive oil

8 ounces frozen artichoke hearts, defrosted

3 cloves garlic, minced

1 medium onion, minced

2 tablespoons capote capers

28 ounces canned crushed tomatoes

1. Heat the oil in a nonstick skillet. Sauté the artichokes, garlic, and onions until the onions are translucent and most of the liquid has evaporated. Put the mixture into a 4-quart slow cooker. Stir in the capers and crushed tomatoes.

2. Cook on high for 4 hours or on low for 8.

PER SERVING Calories: 120 | Fat: 2g | Sodium: 420mg | Carbohydrates: 24g | Fiber: 7g | Protein: 6g

Cleaning Slow Cookers

Do not use very abrasive tools or cleansers on a slow cooker insert. They may scratch the surface, allowing bacteria and food to leach in. Use a soft sponge and baking soda for stubborn stains.

Summer Berry Sauce

Drizzle this sauce over desserts, breakfast foods, even oatmeal.

INGREDIENTS | **SERVES 20**

1 cup raspberries

1 cup blackberries

1 cup golden raspberries

½ cup water

½ teaspoon sugar

Place all ingredients into a 2-quart slow cooker. Lightly mash the berries with the back of a spoon. Cook on low for 2 hours, then uncover and turn on high for ½ hour.

PER SERVING Calories: 10 | Fat: 0g | Sodium: 0mg | Carbohydrates: 2g | Fiber: 1g | Protein: 0g

Pink Tomato Sauce

Try this creamier version of classic spaghetti sauce over linguine or fettuccini.

INGREDIENTS | SERVES 8

1 tablespoon olive oil

1 large onion, diced

2 cloves garlic, minced

1 tablespoon minced fresh basil

1 tablespoon minced fresh Italian parsley

⅔ cup fat-free evaporated milk

1 stalk celery, diced

16 ounces canned whole tomatoes in purée

28 ounces canned crushed tomatoes

Celery, the Star

Celery is often overlooked as an ingredient. It is perfect for slow cooking because it has a high moisture content but still remains crisp through the cooking process. Celery is also very low in calories and high in fiber.

1. Heat the olive oil in a medium-sized nonstick skillet. Sauté the onions and garlic until the onions are soft.

2. Add the onions and garlic to a 6-quart slow cooker. Add the herbs, evaporated milk, celery, and tomatoes. Stir to distribute the spices. Cook on low for 10–12 hours.

PER SERVING Calories: 90 | Fat: 2g | Sodium: 170mg | Carbohydrates: 15g | Fiber: 3g | Protein: 4g

Fennel and Caper Sauce

Try this sauce over boneless pork chops or boneless, skinless chicken breasts and egg noodles.

INGREDIENTS | SERVES 4

2 fennel bulbs with fronds, thinly sliced

2 tablespoons nonpareil capers

½ cup Chicken Stock (page 17)

2 shallots, thinly sliced

2 cups diced fresh tomatoes

¼ teaspoon salt

½ teaspoon freshly ground black pepper

⅓ cup fresh minced parsley

Place the fennel, capers, stock, shallots, tomatoes, salt, and pepper in an oval 4-quart slow cooker. Cook on low for 2 hours, and then add the parsley. Cook an additional 15–30 minutes on high.

PER SERVING Calories: 100 | Fat: 1g | Sodium: 390mg | Carbohydrates: 21g | Fiber: 5g | Protein: 4g

Tomato and Chicken Sausage Sauce

Sausage is a delicious alternative to meatballs in this rich tomato sauce.

INGREDIENTS | SERVES 6

4 Italian chicken sausages, sliced

2 tablespoons tomato paste

28 ounces canned crushed tomatoes

3 cloves garlic, minced

1 onion, minced

3 tablespoons minced basil

1 tablespoon minced Italian parsley

¼ teaspoon crushed rosemary

¼ teaspoon freshly ground black pepper

1. Quickly brown the sausage slices on both sides in a nonstick skillet. Drain any grease. Add the sausages to a 4-quart slow cooker, along with the remaining ingredients. Stir.

2. Cook on low for 8 hours.

PER SERVING Calories: 80 | Fat: 2g | Sodium: 320mg | Carbohydrates: 14g | Fiber: 3g | Protein: 4g

Chicken Meatball Sun-Dried Tomato Sauce

Sun-dried tomatoes make this sauce taste rich without adding fat.

INGREDIENTS | SERVES 6

1 pound ground chicken

½ cup bread crumbs

1 egg

2 cloves garlic, minced

1 shallot, minced

28 ounces crushed tomatoes

½ cup julienne-cut dry (not oil-packed) sun-dried tomatoes

1 onion, minced

1 tablespoon minced fresh basil

The Scoop on Sun-Dried Tomatoes

These tomatoes have been dried in the sun until most of their moisture content has evaporated. Despite losing so much moisture, sun-dried tomatoes retain all of the nutritional benefits of fresh tomatoes, making them a good source of vitamin C and lycopene. Their flavor is more concentrated than fresh tomatoes.

1. Preheat the oven to 375°F. Line two baking sheets with parchment paper. In a large bowl, use your hands to mix the chicken, bread crumbs, egg, and minced garlic and shallot. Form into 1" balls. Place on the baking sheets and bake for 15 minutes or until cooked through.

2. Pour the tomatoes into a 4-quart slow cooker. Add the sun-dried tomatoes, onion, and basil. Stir. Add the meatballs and stir to coat with sauce. Cook on low for 6 hours.

PER SERVING Calories: 220 | Fat: 8g | Sodium: 400mg | Carbohydrates: 23g | Fiber: 4g | Protein: 18g

Chipotle Tomato Sauce

*Try this Southwestern take on the classic Italian tomato sauce
on pasta, or in place of salsa in burritos or tacos.*

INGREDIENTS | **SERVES 6**

3 cloves garlic, minced

1 onion, minced

28 ounces canned crushed tomatoes

14 ounces canned diced tomatoes

3 chipotle peppers in adobo, minced

1 teaspoon dried oregano

1 tablespoon minced cilantro

½ teaspoon freshly ground black pepper

Place all ingredients into a 4-quart slow cooker. Cook on low 8–10 hours. Stir before serving.

PER SERVING Calories: 70 | Fat: 0.5g | Sodium: 390mg | Carbohydrates: 16g | Fiber: 5g | Protein: 3g

Know Your Slow Cooker

When using a new or new-to-you slow cooker for the first time, pick a day when someone can be there to keep tabs on it. In general, older slow cookers cook at a higher temperature than new models, but even new slow cookers can have some differences. It is a good idea to know the quirks of a particular slow cooker so food is not overcooked or undercooked. Tweak cooking times accordingly.

Bolognese Sauce

Also called Bolognese or ragù alla Bolognese, this sauce combines vegetables and meat to create the perfect sauce for pouring over spaghetti.

INGREDIENTS | SERVES 6

2 teaspoons olive oil

½ pound 94% lean ground beef

½ pound ground pork

1 onion, minced

1 carrot, minced

1 stalk celery, minced

3 ounces tomato paste

28 ounces canned diced tomatoes

½ cup fat-free evaporated milk

¼ teaspoon ground black pepper

¼ teaspoon salt

⅛ teaspoon nutmeg

1. Heat the oil in a nonstick pan. Brown the ground beef and pork. Drain off any excess fat.

2. Add the meats and remaining ingredients to a 4-quart slow cooker. Cook on low for 8–10 hours. Stir before serving.

PER SERVING Calories: 240 | Fat: 12g | Sodium: 350mg | Carbohydrates: 16g | Fiber: 4g | Protein: 18g

CHAPTER 8

Beef

Lean Roast with Fennel and Rutabaga

Serve with roasted potatoes.

INGREDIENTS | **SERVES 4**

1 pound rutabaga
2 pounds boneless bottom round roast
½ teaspoon salt
½ teaspoon ground black pepper
1 Vidalia or other sweet onion, sliced
2 bulbs fennel, sliced

Internal Temperatures for Beef

Beef must reach a specific internal temperature, depending on your preference: medium rare, 145°F; medium, 160°F; and well done, 170°F. Use a probe thermometer to determine the internal temperature before you shut off the slow cooker.

1. Peel and cube the rutabaga. Cut any excess fat off the roast. Sprinkle the salt and pepper on all sides of the roast.

2. Heat a nonstick skillet for 30 seconds. Place the roast in the pan. Quickly sear each side of the roast, approximately 5 seconds per side.

3. Place the roast in a 4-quart slow cooker. Cover it with the onions, rutabaga, and fennel.

4. Cook on low for 6 hours or until desired doneness.

PER SERVING Calories: 450 | Fat: 18g | Sodium: 520mg | Carbohydrates: 21g | Fiber: 7g | Protein: 51g

Stuffed Cabbage

This is a wonderful dish to serve to guests. Although there is some preparation to do, you will have plenty of time to clean up before your guests arrive.

INGREDIENTS | **SERVES 4**

Water, as needed

1 large head cabbage

1 teaspoon butter

½ cup sliced onions

28 ounces canned whole tomatoes in purée

½ cup minced onions

1 egg

1½ cups cooked long-grain rice

½ tablespoon garlic powder

½ tablespoon paprika

1 pound 94% lean ground beef

1. Bring a large pot of water to boil. Meanwhile, using a knife, make 4 or 5 cuts around the core of the cabbage and remove the core. Discard the core and 2 layers of the outer leaves. Peel off 6–8 large whole leaves. Place the leaves in a steamer basket and allow them to steam over the boiling water for 7 minutes. Allow the leaves to cool enough to handle. Dice the remaining cabbage to equal ½ cup.

2. In a nonstick skillet, melt butter. Add sliced onions and diced cabbage, and sauté until the onions are soft. Add tomatoes. Break up tomatoes into small chunks using the back of a spoon. Simmer about 10–15 minutes. Ladle one-third of the sauce over the bottom of a 4-quart oval slow cooker.

3. Place the minced onions, egg, rice, spices, and beef into a medium-sized bowl. Stir to distribute all ingredients evenly.

4. Place a cabbage leaf with the open-side up and the stem part facing you on a clean work area. Add about ¼ cup filling to the leaf toward the stem. Fold the sides together, and then pull the top down and over the filling to form a packet. It should look like a burrito. Repeat until all the filling is gone.

5. Arrange the cabbage rolls, seam-side down, in a single layer in the slow cooker. Ladle about half of the remaining sauce over the rolls and repeat with a second layer. Ladle the remaining sauce over the rolls. Cover and cook on low for up to 10 hours.

PER SERVING Calories: 370 | Fat: 8g | Sodium: 150mg | Carbohydrates: 47g | Fiber: 10g | Protein: 33g

Cottage Pie with Carrots, Parsnips, and Celery

Cottage Pie is similar to the more familiar Shepherd's Pie, but it uses beef instead of lamb. This version uses lots of vegetables and lean meat.

INGREDIENTS | SERVES 6

1 large onion, diced

3 cloves garlic, minced

1 carrot, diced

1 parsnip, diced

1 stalk celery, diced

1 pound 94% lean ground beef

1½ cups beef stock

½ teaspoon hot paprika

½ teaspoon crushed rosemary

1 tablespoon Worcestershire sauce

½ teaspoon dried savory

⅛ teaspoon salt

¼ teaspoon freshly ground black pepper

1 tablespoon cornstarch and 1 tablespoon water, mixed (if necessary)

¼ cup minced fresh parsley

2¾ cups plain mashed potatoes

Save Time in the Morning

Take a few minutes the night before cooking to cut up any vegetables you need for a recipe. Place them in an airtight container or plastic bag and refrigerate until morning. Measure any dried spices and place them in a small container on the counter until needed.

1. Sauté the onions, garlic, carrots, parsnips, celery, and beef in a large nonstick skillet until the ground beef is browned. Drain off any excess fat and discard it. Place the mixture into a round 4-quart slow cooker. Add the stock, paprika, rosemary, Worcestershire sauce, savory, salt, and pepper. Stir.

2. Cook on low for 6–8 hours. If the meat mixture still looks very wet, create a slurry by mixing together 1 tablespoon cornstarch and 1 tablespoon water. Stir this into the meat mixture.

3. In a medium bowl, mash the parsley and potatoes using a potato masher. Spread on top of the ground beef mixture in the slow cooker. Cover and cook on high for 30–60 minutes or until the potatoes are warmed through.

PER SERVING Calories: 240 | Fat: 6g | Sodium: 420mg | Carbohydrates: 26g | Fiber: 2g | Protein: 21g

Rouladen

Rouladen is a German dish that has many variations; this one is simply delicious!

INGREDIENTS | SERVES 4

¼ cup red wine

1 cup water

4 very thin round steaks (about ¾ pound total)

2 tablespoons grainy German-style mustard

1 tablespoon lean bacon crumbles (optional)

4 dill pickle spears

Roulade Rules

Roulade, the generic term for steak wrapped around a savory filling, works best with steaks that are approximately ⅛" thick, 8"–10" long, and 5" wide. Look for them in the meat section labeled as "rolling steaks," or ask the butcher to specially cut some. They are a great way to enjoy red meat in small portions.

1. Pour the wine and water into the bottom of an oval 4-quart slow cooker.

2. Place the steaks horizontally on a platter. Spread ½ tablespoon mustard on each steak and sprinkle with one-quarter of the bacon crumbles. Place one of the pickle spears on one end of each steak. Roll each steak toward the other end, so it looks like a spiral. Place on a skillet seam-side down. Cook for 1 minute, then use tongs to flip the steaks carefully and cook the other side for 1 minute.

3. Place each roll in a single layer in the water-wine mixture. Cook on low for 1 hour. Remove the rolls, discarding the cooking liquid.

PER SERVING Calories: 180 | Fat: 7g | Sodium: 970mg | Carbohydrates: 7g | Fiber: <1g | Protein: 20g

Slimmed-Down Moussaka

This version of moussaka uses lean beef instead of higher-fat lamb, baked eggplant instead of fried, and a lighter version of béchamel sauce to create a dish that is authentic tasting but much lower in fat.

INGREDIENTS | SERVES 6

2 1-pound eggplants, peeled
Salt, as needed
1 teaspoon olive oil
1 large onion, diced
2 cloves garlic, minced
20 ounces whole tomatoes in purée
1 tablespoon tomato paste
½ teaspoon cinnamon
1 tablespoon minced oregano
1 tablespoon minced flat-leaf parsley
1 pound 94% lean ground beef
1 cup fat-free evaporated milk
1 tablespoon butter
1 egg
2 tablespoons flour

Slow Cooking with Eggplant

Salting eggplant draws out any extra liquid that might dilute the dish. It is not necessary to salt eggplant in all recipes, but if it is called for, don't skip that step. Similarly, some dishes will call for baking the eggplant. This also helps to dry out the eggplant and ensures a velvety texture.

1. Slice the eggplants vertically into ¼"-thick slices. Place in a colander and lightly salt the eggplant. Allow to drain for 15 minutes. Meanwhile, preheat the oven to 375°F. Rinse off the eggplant slices and pat them dry. Arrange the slices in a single layer on two parchment paper–lined baking sheets. Bake for 15 minutes.

2. While prepping the eggplant, heat the oil in a nonstick skillet. Sauté the onion and garlic for 1 minute, then add the tomatoes, tomato paste, cinnamon, oregano, parsley, and ground beef. Break up the tomatoes into small chunks using the back of a spoon. Simmer, stirring occasionally, until the meat is browned and most of the liquid evaporates.

3. Ladle half of the sauce onto the bottom of a 4- or 6-quart oval slow cooker. Top with a single layer of eggplant, taking care to leave no gaps between slices. Top with remaining sauce. Top with another layer of eggplant. Cover with the lid and cook for 2½–3 hours on high or up to 6 hours on low.

4. In a small saucepan, whisk together the evaporated milk, butter, egg, and flour. Bring to a boil and then reduce the heat. Whisk until smooth.

5. Pour the sauce over the eggplant and cook an additional 1–1½ hours on high.

PER SERVING Calories: 250 | Fat: 8g | Sodium: 150mg | Carbohydrates: 24g | Fiber: 7g | Protein: 24g

Better-Than-Takeout Mongolian Beef

This homemade version of the Chinese takeout favorite is lower in fat and sodium.
Serve it over rice and sprinkle with diced green onion before serving.

INGREDIENTS | SERVES 6

3 pounds lean beef bottom roast, extra fat removed

3 cloves garlic, grated

1" knob peeled fresh ginger, grated

1 medium onion, thinly sliced

½ cup water

½ cup low sodium soy sauce

2 tablespoons black vinegar

2 tablespoons hoisin sauce

1 tablespoon five-spice powder

1 tablespoon cornstarch

1 teaspoon red pepper flakes

1 teaspoon sesame oil

1. Place all ingredients in a 4-quart oval slow cooker. Cover and cook for 5 hours on low or until the meat is thoroughly cooked through and tender.

2. Remove the roast to a cutting board. Slice thinly and return it to the slow cooker. Cook for an additional 20 minutes on high. Stir the meat and the sauce before serving.

PER SERVING Calories: 490 | Fat: 27g | Sodium: 930mg | Carbohydrates: 10g | Fiber: <1g | Protein: 49g

Sauerbraten

This regional dish from Baltimore has a sweet and pickled taste that is uniquely satisfying.

INGREDIENTS | SERVES 8

1 teaspoon whole allspice

1 teaspoon mustard seeds

2 tablespoons whole black peppercorns

1 bay leaf

3 whole cloves

1¾ cups red wine vinegar

½ cup apple cider vinegar

1 teaspoon salt

1 tablespoon sugar

3½ pounds top round roast

2 onions, sliced

2 carrots, sliced

6 reduced-fat gingersnap cookies

Baltimore-Style Potato Dumplings

In a large bowl, mix 4 cups plain mashed potatoes, 3 cups flour, ¾ teaspoon baking powder, 1 egg, and a pinch salt until a dough forms. Bring a large pot of water to a boil and add ice-cream scoops of dough to the water. Boil until they float to the top, about 5 minutes.

1. Place the allspice, mustard seeds, peppercorns, bay leaf, and cloves in cheesecloth. Tie it closed with kitchen twine. Place it into a large resealable plastic bag. Add the vinegars, salt, sugar, and meat. Marinate overnight.

2. The next day place the entire contents of the bag along with the onions and carrots into a 4-quart slow cooker. Cook on low for 8–10 hours. During the last 30 minutes of cooking time, skim off any visible fat that may have risen to the top. Remove the bag of spices, add the gingersnaps, and turn the heat to high.

3. After the time is up, break the meat into chunks using a serving spoon. Serve hot, with dumplings on the side.

PER SERVING Calories: 330 | Fat: 9g | Sodium: 510mg | Carbohydrates: 26g | Fiber: 2g | Protein: 44g

Tamale Pie

In a slight variation from the baked classic, this version of tamale pie features plump, moist cornmeal dumplings.

INGREDIENTS | SERVES 4

1 large onion, minced

1 pound 94% lean ground beef

1 jalapeño, minced

2 cloves garlic, minced

15 ounces canned diced tomatoes

10 ounces canned diced tomatoes with green chiles

15 ounces canned dark red kidney beans, drained and rinsed

4 chipotle peppers in adobo, minced

½ teaspoon hot Mexican chili powder

⅔ cup 2% milk

2 tablespoons canola oil

2 teaspoons baking powder

½ cup cornmeal

½ teaspoon salt

1. Sauté the onion, ground beef, jalapeño, and garlic until the ground beef is browned. Drain off any excess fat.

2. Pour the ground beef mixture into a 4-quart slow cooker. Add the tomatoes, beans, chipotle, and chili powder. Cook on low for 8 hours.

3. In a medium bowl, mix the milk, oil, baking powder, cornmeal, and salt. Drop in ¼-cup mounds in a single layer on top of the beef. Cover and cook on high for 20 minutes without lifting the lid. The dumplings will look fluffy and light when fully cooked.

PER SERVING Calories: 460 | Fat: 15g | Sodium: 1,300mg | Carbohydrates: 47g | Fiber: 11g | Protein: 36g

Canned versus Fresh Tomatoes

While fresh tomatoes are delicious, canned tomatoes are a better choice in some recipes because they have already been cooked. Skins and seeds have been removed from canned tomatoes, which is also a bonus when seeds and skin might detract from the dish. There is also reason to believe that canned tomatoes are better sources of cancer-preventing lycopene simply because they are cooked, and that one can of crushed tomatoes or sauce is the equivalent of dozens of tomatoes.

Beef and Guinness Stew

This stew is filled with vegetables and is very flavorful. The small amounts of sugar and cocoa eliminate the bitterness occasionally found in similar stews without being detectable.

INGREDIENTS | SERVES 8

2 teaspoons canola oil

1 large onion, diced

2 parsnips, diced

2 carrots, diced

2 stalks celery, diced

3 cloves garlic, minced

2 russet potatoes, diced

2 tablespoons minced fresh rosemary

2 pounds lean top round roast, cut into 1" cubes

1 tablespoon dark brown sugar

¼ teaspoon salt

½ teaspoon freshly ground black pepper

1 tablespoon baking cocoa

1 cup water

½ cup Guinness extra stout

½ cup frozen peas

1. Heat the oil in a large skillet. Sauté the onions, parsnips, carrots, celery, garlic, potatoes, rosemary, and beef until the ingredients begin to soften and brown. Drain any excess fat.

2. Add to a 4-quart slow cooker. Sprinkle with sugar, salt, pepper, and cocoa. Pour in the water and Guinness. Stir. Cook for 8–9 hours on low.

3. Add the frozen peas. Cover and cook an additional ½ hour on high. Stir before serving.

PER SERVING Calories: 230 | Fat: 5g | Sodium: 170mg | Carbohydrates: 25g | Fiber: 4g | Protein: 27g

Choosing Cuts of Beef

Leaner cuts like top round are excellent choices for slow cooking because the long cooking time tenderizes them. Look for cuts that have minimal marbling and trim off any excess fat before cooking. Searing and sautéing are good ways to cook off some external fat before adding the meat to the slow cooker. Drain any excess fat.

Ropa Vieja

Serve this Cuban dish with yellow rice and Cuban Black Beans (page 204).

INGREDIENTS | SERVES 8

2 pounds top round roast

1 cubanelle pepper, diced

1 large onion, diced

2 carrots, diced

28 ounces canned crushed tomatoes

2 cloves garlic

1 tablespoon oregano

½ teaspoon cumin

½ cup sliced green olives stuffed with pimento

1. Place the roast, pepper, onions, carrots, tomatoes, garlic, oregano, and cumin into a 2-quart slow cooker. Cook on high for 7 hours. Add the olives and continue to cook for 20 minutes.

2. Shred the meat with a fork, then mash it with a potato masher until very well mixed.

PER SERVING Calories: 260 | Fat: 11g | Sodium: 460mg | Carbohydrates: 13g | Fiber: 3g | Protein: 27g

Corned Beef and Cabbage

This slimmed-down version of corned beef and cabbage has more vegetables and slightly less meat but all of the flavor of the classic dish.

INGREDIENTS | SERVES 6

¾ pound corned beef brisket

1 head green cabbage, cut into wedges

2 carrots, sliced

2 parsnips, sliced

2 cups water

1 onion, sliced

1 teaspoon yellow mustard seeds

1. Trim excess fat off the brisket. Cut into 1" cubes.

2. Add the brisket and all of the remaining ingredients to a 4-quart slow cooker. Cook on low for 10 hours.

PER SERVING Calories: 270 | Fat: 13g | Sodium: 95mg | Carbohydrates: 24g | Fiber: 7g | Protein: 14g

Winter Borscht

*Winter Borscht is a heartier version of Summer Borscht (page 62)
and is served hot. Try it with a dollop of sour cream.*

INGREDIENTS | SERVES 6

¾ pound cubed lean top round beef

3½ cups shredded "Roasted" Beets
(page 188)

1 onion, diced

1 carrot, grated

½ teaspoon salt

½ teaspoon sugar

3 tablespoons red wine vinegar

½ teaspoon freshly ground black pepper

½ tablespoon dill seed

1 clove garlic, minced

1 cup shredded green cabbage

2 cups Roasted Vegetable Stock (page
19) or beef broth

2 cups water

1. In a nonstick skillet, sauté the beef for 1 minute. Drain off any excess fat.

2. Place the beef and the remaining ingredients into a 4-quart slow cooker. Cook on low for 8 hours. Stir before serving.

PER SERVING Calories: 120 | Fat: 4g | Sodium: 340mg | Carbohydrates: 7g | Fiber: 2g | Protein: 14g

Red Wine Pot Roast

A little bit of wine goes a long way in flavoring this simple one-crock meal. Using lean meat ensures grease-free vegetables.

INGREDIENTS | SERVES 6

⅓ cup red wine

½ cup water

4 red skin potatoes, quartered

3 carrots, cut into thirds

2 bulbs fennel, quartered

2 rutabagas, quartered

1 onion, sliced

4 cloves garlic, sliced

1½ pounds lean top round roast, excess fat removed

½ teaspoon salt

½ teaspoon freshly ground black pepper

1. Pour the wine and water into an oval 4-quart slow cooker. Add the potatoes, carrots, fennel, rutabagas, onions, and garlic. Stir.

2. Add the beef. Sprinkle with salt and pepper. Cook on low for 8 hours.

3. Remove and slice the beef. Use a slotted spoon to serve the vegetables. Discard the cooking liquid.

PER SERVING Calories: 320 | Fat: 4g | Sodium: 350mg | Carbohydrates: 45g | Fiber: 9g | Protein: 30g

Taco Filling

Smoky hot chipotle peppers give this filling a rich spicy flavor. Try it with soft whole-grain tortillas and topped with lettuce, avocado, and tomato.

INGREDIENTS | SERVES 8

1½ pounds 94% lean ground beef
1 onion, minced
15 ounces canned fire-roasted diced tomatoes
1 Anaheim pepper, minced
2 chipotle peppers in adobo, minced
½ teaspoon cumin
½ teaspoon cayenne pepper
½ teaspoon paprika
½ teaspoon garlic powder
½ teaspoon oregano

1. Sauté the beef and onion in a nonstick skillet until just browned. Drain off any grease. Add to a 4-quart slow cooker. Break up any large pieces of beef with a spoon.

2. Add the remaining ingredients and stir. Cook on low for 7 hours. Stir prior to serving.

PER SERVING Calories: 140 | Fat: 4.5g | Sodium: 80mg | Carbohydrates: 4g | Fiber: 1g | Protein: 19g

Skinny French Dip Beef for Sandwiches

The long cooking time makes lean meat fork-tender, perfect for stuffing into crusty bread for sandwiches.

INGREDIENTS | SERVES 8

2 pounds lean bottom round roast
1 Vidalia or Walla Walla onion, sliced
2 cloves garlic, sliced
3 tablespoons soy sauce
1 tablespoon minced fresh thyme
1 teaspoon minced fresh rosemary
1 teaspoon freshly ground black pepper

1. Slice the beef into rounds, removing excess fat. Place into a 4-quart slow cooker. Add the remaining ingredients.

2. Cook 10 hours or until the meat is falling apart. Shred with a fork.

PER SERVING Calories: 160 | Fat: 5g | Sodium: 440mg | Carbohydrates: 3g | Fiber: 0g | Protein: 26g

Beef Biryani

Biryani is a one-dish meal that is well spiced but not spicy. Traditionally it is made using ghee, a type of clarified butter, but slow cooking brings out the flavor without adding fat.

INGREDIENTS | SERVES 6

1 pound top round, cut into strips
1 tablespoon minced fresh ginger
½ teaspoon ground cloves
½ teaspoon ground cardamom
½ teaspoon ground coriander
½ teaspoon freshly ground black pepper
½ teaspoon cinnamon
½ teaspoon cumin
¼ teaspoon salt
2 cloves garlic, minced
1 onion, minced
1 cup fat-free Greek yogurt
1 cup frozen peas
1½ cups cooked basmati or brown rice

1. Place the beef, spices, garlic, and onion into a 4-quart slow cooker. Stir. Cook for 7–8 hours.

2. About 30 minutes before serving, stir in the yogurt, peas, and rice. Cook for 30 minutes. Stir before serving.

PER SERVING Calories: 230 | Fat: 7g | Sodium: 190mg | Carbohydrates: 20g | Fiber: 2g | Protein: 21g

Beef Rogan Josh

*Traditionally made with lamb, this lean-beef version is lower in fat but
full of flavor. Serve it over rice with pappadums on the side.*

INGREDIENTS | SERVES 6

1 pound cubed bottom round
1 onion, diced
4 cloves garlic, minced
2 tablespoons cumin
2 tablespoons coriander
1 tablespoon turmeric
2 teaspoons cardamom
2 teaspoons minced fresh ginger
2 teaspoons freshly ground black pepper
2 teaspoons chili powder
28 ounces crushed tomatoes
1 cup fat-free Greek yogurt

1. In a nonstick skillet, sauté the beef, onion, and garlic until just browned. Drain off any excess fat. Place into a 4-quart slow cooker.

2. Add the spices and crushed tomatoes. Cook on low for 8 hours. Stir in the yogurt prior to serving.

PER SERVING Calories: 230 | Fat: 10g | Sodium: 250mg | Carbohydrates: 18g | Fiber: 4g | Protein: 20g

CHAPTER 9

Pork

Apples-and-Onions Pork Chops

Try Sonya apples in this sweet and savory dish; they are crisp and sweet.

INGREDIENTS | SERVES 4

4 crisp, sweet apples

2 large onions, sliced

4 thick cut boneless pork chops (about 1 pound)

½ teaspoon ground cayenne

½ teaspoon ground cinnamon

¼ teaspoon allspice

¼ teaspoon ground fennel

Slow Cooking with Boneless Pork

Not only is there less waste associated with boneless pork chops or roasts, there is often less fat attached to the meat. Even without much fat, boneless pork is well suited to slow cooking. All of the moisture stays in the dish, ensuring tender pork.

1. Cut the apples into wedges. Place half of the wedges in the bottom of an oval 4-quart slow cooker along with half of the sliced onions. Top with a single layer of pork chops. Sprinkle with spices, and top with the remaining apples and onions.

2. Cook on low for 8 hours.

PER SERVING Calories: 340 | Fat: 10g | Sodium: 75mg | Carbohydrates: 30g | Fiber: 6g | Protein: 35g

Georgia-Style Pulled Pork

Serve on large buns and top with coleslaw.

INGREDIENTS | **SERVES 8**

3½ pounds boneless pork roast

1 cup Homemade Barbecue Sauce (see page 100)

1 large onion, diced

2 cloves garlic, minced

1 tablespoon hickory liquid smoke

1 jalapeño, sliced

Quick Coleslaw

Gather 16 ounces coleslaw mix (shredded cabbages and carrot), ¼ cup mayonnaise, ½ teaspoon celery seed, 1¼ cups apple cider vinegar, ¼ cup thinly sliced onion. Toss ingredients and refrigerate for 1 hour before serving.

1. Place all ingredients into a 4-quart slow cooker. Cook on low for 8 hours or until the meat is easily shredded with a fork.

2. Remove the pork from the slow cooker to a plate. Shred the meat with a fork. Mash the remaining sauce and solids in the slow cooker with a potato masher until fairly smooth. Add the pork back to the slow cooker and toss to coat in the sauce.

PER SERVING Calories: 410 | Fat: 18g | Sodium: 140mg | Carbohydrates: 2g | Fiber: 0g | Protein: 55g

Pork with Caramelized Onions, Roasted Potatoes, and Apples

Caramelized onions add a touch of sweetness to this dish.

INGREDIENTS | SERVES 10

5 pounds boneless pork roast

1 cup Caramelized Onions (page 16)

1 pound baby red skin potatoes

2 apples, cored and sliced

¼ cup water

¼ cup balsamic vinegar

1 teaspoon paprika

¼ teaspoon freshly ground pepper

¼ teaspoon ground cinnamon

⅛ teaspoon salt

Countertop Caution

The bottoms of ceramic slow cooker inserts are unfinished and may scratch stone or marble countertops. Leave them on towels to air-dry before returning them to their bases.

1. Trim extra fat from the roast. Quickly sear it on all sides in a hot nonstick pan.

2. Place the roast in a 4-quart oval slow cooker. Top with the onions, potatoes, and apples. Add the water and vinegar; then sprinkle with the spices.

3. Cover and cook on low for 8 hours or until the pork is tender and falling apart.

PER SERVING Calories: 540 | Fat: 21g | Sodium: 180mg | Carbohydrates: 19g | Fiber: 2g | Protein: 64g

Chinese-Style Boneless Ribs

Boneless pork ribs may also be labeled "country-style ribs" or "Southern-style ribs."

INGREDIENTS | SERVES 4

1 teaspoon canola oil

2 pounds boneless pork ribs

2 cloves minced garlic

1 tablespoon red pepper flakes

1 small onion, minced

1 tablespoon five-spice powder

1 tablespoon black vinegar

¼ cup soy sauce

2 tablespoons lime juice

1 teaspoon sesame oil

1. Heat the oil in a large skillet. Cook the pork for 1 minute on each side. Place in a 4-quart slow cooker. Pour the remaining ingredients over the meat. Cover and cook on low for 8 hours.

2. If the sauce is very thin, pour into a saucepan and cook until it reduces. Drizzle the sauce on the ribs and serve.

PER SERVING Calories: 530 | Fat: 26g | Sodium: 115mg | Carbohydrates: 7g | Fiber: <1g | Protein: 64g

Easy Homemade Five Spice Powder

Mix 1 teaspoon each of cinnamon, star anise, cloves, ground ginger, and ground Sichuan peppercorns. If you can't find the peppercorns, use fennel. Store in an airtight container.

Smoky Mango Pulled Pork

Serve this on big crusty rolls.

INGREDIENTS | SERVES 6

2½ pounds boneless pork roast, excess fat trimmed

1 mango, cubed

¼ cup chile sauce

¼ cup balsamic vinegar

1 tablespoon yellow hot sauce

1 teaspoon ground cayenne

1 teaspoon freshly ground black pepper

1 large onion, thinly sliced

1 teaspoon liquid smoke

3 cloves garlic, minced

1 teaspoon hot Mexican chili powder

1 habanero pepper, minced

2 tablespoons lime juice

1. Place all ingredients in a 4-quart slow cooker. Cook on low for 8–9 hours or on high for 6 hours.

2. When it is done, the meat should shred easily with a fork. Remove the roast from the slow cooker. Use two forks to shred the pork; set it aside. Mash any solid bits of the sauce in the slow cooker with a potato masher. Return the pork to the slow cooker, and toss to coat the meat evenly.

PER SERVING Calories: 440 | Fat: 17g | Sodium: 320mg | Carbohydrates: 16g | Fiber: 1g | Protein: 53g

Cooking with Hot Peppers

Before using hot peppers, remove the stems. If you want the final product to have a smooth texture, remove the seeds as well. Wear gloves when cutting up hot peppers to avoid accidentally transferring the burning oils to your eyes or skin.

Pork Adobada

*Adobada is Spanish for marinated, but you can achieve a similar effect
by cooking the pork loin for a very long time over low heat.*

INGREDIENTS | SERVES 8

1 teaspoon canola oil

3 pounds pork loin

1 medium onion, diced

5 cloves garlic, minced

1½ cups water

½ cup apple cider vinegar

¼ cup orange juice

3 tablespoons light brown sugar

1 tablespoon ground cumin

1 tablespoon ground Anaheim chile

1 teaspoon ground cayenne

1. Heat the oil in a large skillet. Cook the pork for 1 minute on each side. Place it in a 4-quart slow cooker, and pour the remaining ingredients over the meat. Cover and cook on low for 6 hours.

2. If the sauce is very thin, pour it into a saucepan and cook until it reduces. Pour the sauce over the roast and shred the meat with a fork. Toss to distribute the sauce evenly over the meat.

PER SERVING Calories: 430 | Fat: 23g | Sodium: 120mg | Carbohydrates: 10g | Fiber: <1g | Protein: 43g

Pork Sausages Braised in Sauerkraut

This is a great meal for a party; the sausages can be kept warm for hours without overcooking.

INGREDIENTS | SERVES 6

6 reduced-fat smoked pork sausages

4 pounds sauerkraut

½ tablespoon caraway seeds

1 tablespoon yellow mustard seeds

1 small onion, thinly sliced

2 tablespoons apple cider vinegar

1. Prick each sausage with a fork at least once. Quickly sear in a dry skillet to brown all sides for about 1 minute. Remove from the skillet and cut a slit down the middle of each sausage vertically ¼" deep.

2. Place the sauerkraut, caraway seeds, mustard seeds, onions, and vinegar into a 4- or 6-quart slow cooker. Stir to distribute all ingredients evenly.

3. Add the sausage. Toss. Cover and cook for 3–4 hours on low.

PER SERVING Calories: 100 | Fat: 3.5g | Sodium: 2,070mg | Carbohydrates: 15g | Fiber: 8g | Protein: 5g

Red Cooked Pork

Red Cooked Pork, although not red at all, is an excellent example of home-style Chinese cooking. Serve with rice and steamed vegetables.

INGREDIENTS | SERVES 6

1½ pounds boneless pork loin
¼ cup Shaoxing (Chinese cooking wine)
4 cloves garlic
1 cup water
2 tablespoons dark brown sugar
2 tablespoons dark soy sauce
3 whole star anise

How to Braise

Braising is a technique that is well suited to the slow cooker. The first step is to sear the meat to enhance flavor. Then transfer it to the slow cooker to simmer slowly until it is fork-tender.

1. Heat a nonstick skillet. Quickly sear the meat on all sides.

2. Place all ingredients into a 4-quart slow cooker. Stir. Cook on low for 8–9 hours.

3. Remove the roast from the slow cooker and slice or cube. Pour the sauce into a small saucepan and cook until it reduces and thickens. Discard the star anise and drizzle the sauce over the meat.

PER SERVING Calories: 260 | Fat: 9g | Sodium: 470mg | Carbohydrates: 6g | Fiber: 0g | Protein: 35g

Pork Roast with Cranberry Sauce

This pairs wonderfully with Wild Rice with Mixed Vegetables (page 203).

INGREDIENTS | **SERVES 4**

1 medium onion, thinly sliced

1¼ pounds pork loin

2 tablespoons sweetened dried cranberries

1 cup Cranberry Sauce (page 49)

Cooking with Pork Loin

Pork loin is an exceptionally lean cut. If a pork loin does have some excess fat, it can be removed easily before cooking. Another lean cut is the tenderloin roast, which is as lean as skinless chicken breast.

1. Place the onion slices on the bottom of a 4-quart slow cooker. Top with the pork, then the dried cranberries, and finally the cranberry sauce to cover the whole roast.

2. Cover and cook on low for 8 hours. Remove the pork and slice it. Discard the cooking liquids.

PER SERVING Calories: 350 | Fat: 19g | Sodium: 105mg | Carbohydrates: 7g | Fiber: 1g | Protein: 36g

Italian Pork with Cannellini Beans

This is an incredibly simple one-dish meal that is packed with flavor.

INGREDIENTS | **SERVES 4**

1½ pounds pork loin

28 ounces crushed tomatoes

1 head roasted garlic

1 onion, minced

2 tablespoons capers

2 teaspoons Italian-blend herbs

15 ounces canned cannellini beans, drained and rinsed

1. Place the pork loin into a 4-quart slow cooker. Add the tomatoes, garlic, onions, and capers. Cook on low for 7–8 hours.

2. Add the cannellini beans 1 hour before serving and continue to cook on low for the remaining time.

PER SERVING Calories: 510 | Fat: 15g | Sodium: 740mg | Carbohydrates: 34g | Fiber: 8g | Protein: 59g

Tomato-Braised Pork

Here the pork is gently cooked in tomatoes to yield meltingly tender meat.

INGREDIENTS | SERVES 4

28 ounces canned crushed tomatoes

3 tablespoons tomato paste

1 cup loosely packed fresh basil

½ teaspoon freshly ground black pepper

½ teaspoon marjoram

1¼ pounds boneless pork roast

1. Place the tomatoes, tomato paste, basil, pepper, and marjoram into a 4-quart slow cooker. Stir to create a uniform sauce. Add the pork.

2. Cook on low for 7–8 hours or until the pork easily falls apart when poked with a fork.

PER SERVING Calories: 360 | Fat: 13g | Sodium: 450mg | Carbohydrates: 17g | Fiber: 5g | Protein: 43g

Chinese Hot Pot

Using the slow cooker makes this dish easy to try at home.

INGREDIENTS | SERVES 4

1" knob fresh ginger, sliced

1 quart Chicken Stock (page 17)

2½ cups water

2 green onions, diced

¼ pound fresh shiitake mushrooms, sliced

3 cloves garlic

¾ pound very thinly sliced pork

3 heads baby bok choy, chopped

4 ounces enoki mushrooms

4 ounces cellophane noodles

1. Place the ginger, stock, water, onions, shiitake mushrooms, and garlic in a 4-quart slow cooker. Cook on low for 7–8 hours.

2. Add the pork, bok choy, enoki mushrooms, and noodles. Cook on high for 15–30 minutes.

PER SERVING Calories: 470 | Fat: 11g | Sodium: 810mg | Carbohydrates: 54g | Fiber: 8g | Protein: 43g

Southwestern Pork Roast

The flavors of the Southwest make this pork roast special. Try using leftovers as taco filling.

INGREDIENTS | SERVES 6

1½ pounds lean pork roast, excess fat removed

15 ounces canned black beans, drained and rinsed

14 ounces canned diced tomatoes with green chiles

1 teaspoon cayenne pepper

½ teaspoon ground chipotle pepper

1 onion, chopped

3 cloves garlic, minced

2 jalapeños, sliced

1 teaspoon hot sauce

1 tablespoon lime juice

Place the pork in a 4-quart slow cooker. Top with the remaining ingredients. Cook on low for 8 hours or until the pork is fully cooked.

PER SERVING Calories: 330 | Fat: 16g | Sodium: 470mg | Carbohydrates: 17g | Fiber: 5g | Protein: 33g

Sour Cherry–Glazed Pork

Ginger preserves are a short cut to a flavorful sauce without a lot of fuss. Look for ginger preserves near the jams and jellies at any supermarket.

INGREDIENTS | SERVES 4

3 tablespoons ginger preserves

¼ cup dried sour cherries

⅔ cup water

¼ teaspoon freshly ground black pepper

¼ teaspoon salt

⅛ teaspoon ground nutmeg

1¼ pounds pork loin

1. In a small bowl, whisk the preserves, sour cherries, water, pepper, salt, and nutmeg.

2. Place the pork loin into a 4-quart slow cooker. Pour the glaze over the pork. Cook on low for 8 hours.

PER SERVING Calories: 290 | Fat: 15g | Sodium: 210mg | Carbohydrates: 7g | Fiber: 0g | Protein: 30g

Glazed Lean Pork Shoulder

Apples and apple cider form a glaze over a long cooking time that is both flavorful and light. Use crisp, in-season apples for best results.

INGREDIENTS | SERVES 8

3 pounds bone-in pork shoulder, excess fat removed
3 apples, thinly sliced
¼ cup apple cider
1 tablespoon brown sugar
1 teaspoon allspice
½ teaspoon cinnamon
¼ teaspoon nutmeg

Place the pork shoulder into a 4-quart slow cooker. Top with the remaining ingredients. Cook on low for 8 hours. Remove the lid and cook on high for 30 minutes or until the sauce thickens.

PER SERVING Calories: 280 | Fat: 11g | Sodium: 140mg | Carbohydrates: 11g | Fiber: 2g | Protein: 34g

Chinese-Style Braised Pork

This Chinese-inspired pork is perfect served sliced over rice and garnished with chopped green onion.

INGREDIENTS | SERVES 4

1⅓ pounds pork loin
2 cloves minced garlic
1 tablespoon red pepper flakes
1 small onion, minced
1 teaspoon ground ginger
1 teaspoon ground garlic
½ teaspoon cinnamon
½ teaspoon ground star anise
1 tablespoon rice vinegar
3 tablespoons soy sauce
1 teaspoon sesame oil

1. Heat a large nonstick skillet. Cook the pork for 1 minute on each side.

2. Place the pork in a 4-quart slow cooker. Pour the remaining ingredients over the meat. Cover and cook on low 8 hours.

PER SERVING Calories: 340 | Fat: 14g | Sodium: 850mg | Carbohydrates: 5g | Fiber: 1g | Protein: 47g

Boneless Pork Ribs

A fresh but quick homemade barbecue sauce makes all the difference with these ribs. They are flavorful and tender.

INGREDIENTS | SERVES 4

1¼ pounds boneless pork ribs

2 teaspoons ground chipotle

¼ teaspoon salt

1 teaspoon freshly ground black pepper

1 tablespoon ginger juice

2 tablespoons Blackberry Jam (page 189)

½ cup chili sauce

½ tablespoon hickory liquid smoke

½ teaspoon garlic powder

½ teaspoon onion powder

2 tablespoons balsamic vinegar

1 teaspoon Worcestershire sauce

1. Rub both sides of the pork with the chipotle, salt, and pepper. Place into an oval 4-quart slow cooker.

2. In a small bowl, whisk together the remaining ingredients until smooth.

3. Pour the sauce over the ribs. Cook for 6–8 hours.

PER SERVING Calories: 360 | Fat: 15g | Sodium: 600mg | Carbohydrates: 13g | Fiber: <1g | Protein: 40g

How to Make Ginger Juice

Use a fine grater to grate several inches of fresh ginger. Strain to remove any solids. Refrigerate in an airtight container for up to 1 week. Use in place of fresh ginger or in sauces and drinks.

Caribbean Pulled Pork

Serve this Caribbean–Southern fusion pulled pork on sesame seed buns.

INGREDIENTS | SERVES 6

2 pounds pork loin

¼ cup chili sauce

1 Scotch bonnet pepper, minced

¼ cup red wine vinegar

½ teaspoon freshly ground black pepper

1 tablespoon ginger preserves

2 tablespoons orange juice

1 tablespoon lime juice

½ teaspoon allspice

½ teaspoon ground cloves

½ teaspoon cayenne pepper

½ teaspoon oregano

½ teaspoon cumin

½ teaspoon thyme

1 teaspoon hickory liquid smoke

1 onion, chopped

2 cloves garlic

1. Place all ingredients into a 4-quart slow cooker. Cook on low for 8–10 hours or until the pork is easily shredded with a fork.

2. Remove the pork from the slow cooker. Place it on a plate and shred it with a fork. Mash the mixture in the slow cooker with a potato masher. Return the pork to the slow cooker and toss to coat.

PER SERVING Calories: 340 | Fat: 12g | Sodium: 220mg | Carbohydrates: 7g | Fiber: <1g | Protein: 46g

Jamaican Ham

This pleasantly spiced ham is the perfect weekday version of the Jamaican holiday dish.

INGREDIENTS | SERVES 4

20 ounces canned pineapple chunks in juice

1½ pounds boneless smoked ham quarter

1 tablespoon ground cloves

1 teaspoon allspice

1 teaspoon ground ginger

Banish Dull Flavors

Store herbs and spices in a cool, dark cabinet to preserve freshness and flavor. Label each bottle with the date it was opened. Discard 1 year after first use.

1. Use toothpicks to attach half the pineapple chunks to the ham. Place it into a 4-quart slow cooker.

2. Pour the remaining pineapple chunks, juice, and spices over the ham. Cook for 6–8 hours on low.

3. Remove the ham from the slow cooker. Remove the toothpicks, placing the pineapple chunks back into the slow cooker. Stir the contents of the slow cooker.

4. Slice the ham and return it to the slow cooker. Toss with the juices prior to serving.

PER SERVING Calories: 300 | Fat: 4.5g | Sodium: 1,550mg | Carbohydrates: 34g | Fiber: 2g | Protein: 31g

Slow-Cooked Char Siu

Char Siu (Chinese barbecue pork) is excellent in egg rolls, wonton soup, fried rice, and stir fries, and is an integral part of Char Siu Bao (steamed pork buns).

INGREDIENTS | SERVES 6

1½ pounds boneless pork rib, trimmed of excess fat

¼ cup soy sauce

¼ cup hoisin sauce

3 tablespoons Chinese rice wine

2 tablespoons golden syrup

1 tablespoon sesame seed paste or tahini

1 tablespoon grated lime peel

1 teaspoon grated ginger

1 teaspoon minced garlic

1 teaspoon sesame oil

½ teaspoon five-spice powder

2 tablespoons lime juice

1. Slice the pork into 3"-wide strips. Place the pork in a resealable plastic bag. Add the remaining ingredients. Refrigerate overnight.

2. Pour the pork and marinade into a 4-quart slow cooker. Cook on low for 8 hours.

PER SERVING Calories: 330 | Fat: 14g | Sodium: 890mg | Carbohydrates: 13g | Fiber: <1g | Protein: 34g

Pork Roast with Prunes

Pork pairs wonderfully with fruit, and this recipe is no exception. The prunes add richness to the pork that is perfect for autumn.

INGREDIENTS | SERVES 6

1½ pounds lean pork roast, excess fat removed

1 onion, diced

2 cloves garlic, minced

¾ cup pitted prunes

½ cup water

½ teaspoon freshly ground black pepper

¼ teaspoon salt

⅛ teaspoon nutmeg

⅛ teaspoon cinnamon

Place all ingredients into a 4-quart slow cooker. Cook on low for 8 hours.

PER SERVING Calories: 290 | Fat: 10g | Sodium: 170mg | Carbohydrates: 15g | Fiber: 1g | Protein: 32g

Picking Prunes

Prunes are dried plums. They are wrinkly and chewy. Due to their somewhat negative association as a fruit that only the elderly enjoy, they are sometimes marketed as "dried plums."

CHAPTER 10

Poultry

Chicken and Dumplings

Memories of bland chicken and dumplings will be banished forever after one bite of this flavorful Cajun-influenced dish.

INGREDIENTS | SERVES 6

1 tablespoon canola oil
1 onion, chopped
3 cloves garlic, minced
1 cup diced crimini mushrooms
2 carrots, diced
2 stalks celery, diced
1 parsnip, diced
1 jalapeño, seeded and diced
½ teaspoon salt
½ teaspoon ground black pepper
1 large red skin potato, diced
½ teaspoon dried dill weed
½ teaspoon ground cayenne
6 cups Chicken Stock (page 17)
3 cups diced, cooked chicken breast
1 tablespoon baking powder
2 cups flour
¾ cup 1% milk or fat-free buttermilk
2 eggs
¼ cup chopped green onion

1. Heat the canola oil in a small skillet, then add the onions, garlic, and mushrooms. Sauté until softened, about 2 minutes. Add to an oval 4-quart slow cooker along with the carrots, celery, parsnip, jalapeño, salt, pepper, potato, dill weed, cayenne, and stock. Cook on low for 6 hours.

2. Add the cooked chicken and turn up to high.

3. Meanwhile, whisk the baking powder and flour in a medium bowl. Stir in the buttermilk, eggs, and green onion. Mix to combine. Divide the mixture into 3" dumplings.

4. Carefully drop the dumplings one at a time into the slow cooker. Cover and continue to cook on high for 30 minutes or until the dumplings are cooked through and fluffy.

PER SERVING Calories: 490 | Fat: 10g | Sodium: 920mg | Carbohydrates: 63g | Fiber: 5g | Protein: 36g

It's in the Book!

This is a great recipe to use the Chicken Stock (page 17) in. Make the stock the day before or overnight. You could even use leftover chicken from Slow Roasted Chicken with Potatoes, Parsnips, and Onions (page 224). Planning ahead saves time.

Turkey Mole

Despite the number of chiles, this is not a terribly spicy sauce. The chiles add a lot of flavor but not much heat. Look for them in the Mexican or produce section of most grocery stores.

INGREDIENTS | SERVES 8

½ cup pepitas (raw, hulled pumpkin seeds)

5 dried guajillo chiles, stems and seeds removed

5 dried pasilla chiles, stems and seeds removed

4 cups boiling water

4 cloves garlic

1 onion, cut into eighths

1 tablespoon cocoa

1 teaspoon salt

1 teaspoon freshly ground pepper

1 3" stick Mexican cinnamon

1 teaspoon cloves

1 tablespoon oregano

1 6-pound turkey breast

14 ounces canned fire-roasted diced tomatoes

Cooking with Dried Peppers

Dried peppers need to be rehydrated before being used in most recipes. Soak them in boiling water or stock for 15 minutes and then towel them dry before adding them to the cooker to avoid diluting your dish.

1. Place the pepitas and chiles in a dry nonstick pan. Turn the heat to medium and cook, stirring occasionally, until the pepitas start to pop. Using tongs, remove the chiles and place them in a heat-safe bowl. Pour the boiling water over the chiles. Allow them to soak 15 minutes.

2. Scoop the chiles out of the hot water and into a food processor. Reserve the water. Add the pepitas, garlic, onion, cocoa, salt, pepper, cinnamon, cloves, oregano, and ¼ cup of the water used to rehydrate the chiles. Pulse until a smooth paste forms.

3. Place the turkey into an oval 6-quart slow cooker. Add the tomatoes. Spoon the mole sauce over and around the turkey breast. Cook on high for 2 hours, then switch to low for an additional 6 hours.

4. Remove the turkey from the slow cooker. Discard the skin. Pour the sauce through a mesh strainer into a bowl. Discard the liquid in the bowl and retain the solids in the strainer. The solids remaining constitute the mole sauce. Toss the meat with the sauce or serve the sauce on the side.

PER SERVING Calories: 520 | Fat: 6g | Sodium: 490mg | Carbohydrates: 19g | Fiber: 3g | Protein: 89g

Enchilada Filling

This recipe is an excellent way to use up leftover chicken or turkey, and it makes enough filling for two 9" x 13" pans (8 enchiladas per dish) of enchiladas. Make one pan and freeze the other for another time.

INGREDIENTS | SERVES 8

3 jalapeños, halved

1 teaspoon canola oil

1 large onion, diced

3 cloves garlic, minced

1 teaspoon dried oregano

1 teaspoon ground cayenne

½ teaspoon cumin

28 ounces canned crushed tomatoes

¾ cup Chicken Stock (page 17) or Spicy Smoked Turkey Stock (page 20)

1 tablespoon lime juice

4 cups shredded cooked chicken or turkey

1. Place the jalapeños cut-side down on a broiler pan. Broil on low for 2 minutes or until they start to brown. Allow to cool, and then dice.

2. In a nonstick skillet, heat the oil. Add the onions, garlic, and jalapeños, and sauté until the onions are soft, about 5 minutes.

3. Add the onion mixture to a 4-quart slow cooker. Add the remaining spices, crushed tomatoes, stock, and lime juice. Cook on low for 5–6 hours, then add the shredded meat. Turn up to high and cook for an additional hour.

PER SERVING Calories: 170 | Fat: 4g | Sodium: 220mg | Carbohydrates: 11g | Fiber: 3g | Protein: 24g

Don't Overfill

Leave at least an inch of headroom in the slow cooker. The lid needs to fit tightly for the slow cooker to cook properly; otherwise the liquid ingredients may boil over, leaving you with a potentially dangerous situation and quite a mess.

Orange Chicken

Serve this slimmed-down version of orange chicken with rice and steamed broccoli.

INGREDIENTS | SERVES 4

2 tablespoons dark soy sauce

2 tablespoons spiced ginger preserves

½ cup freshly squeezed orange juice

1 large orange, sliced into ⅛"-thick slices

3 boneless, skinless chicken breasts (about ¾ pound)

Cooking with Boneless Skinless Chicken Breasts

Boneless skinless breasts are a low-fat source of protein, but it can be tricky to use them in the slow cooker. They are best when used raw in a recipe with a short cooking time to avoid any chance of drying out. Cooked, they hold up well when added toward the end of a longer cooking recipe such as a soup, stew, or chili.

1. Whisk together the soy sauce, preserves, and juice in a small bowl.

2. Arrange the orange slices along the bottom of a 4-quart slow cooker. Top with the chicken breasts. Pour the sauce over the chicken. Cook for 3 hours on low or until the chicken is thoroughly cooked.

PER SERVING Calories: 170 | Fat: 2.5g | Sodium: 560mg | Carbohydrates: 10g | Fiber: 1g | Protein: 26g

Mushroom Turkey Breast

Serve this with Wild Rice with Mixed Vegetables (page 203) or Rosemary-Garlic Mashed Potatoes (page 199) to help sop up the delicious juices this dish yields.

INGREDIENTS | SERVES 6

1 teaspoon butter

1 medium onion, sliced

8 ounces sliced crimini mushrooms

1½ pounds turkey breast cutlets

1 teaspoon minced fresh sage

⅛ teaspoon salt

¼ teaspoon ground black pepper

¼ cup water

Quick Tip

Make sure that your slow cooker is at least half filled before cooking for best results. If the slow cooker is not filled halfway, the food will cook too quickly and might burn or dry out. Aim for half to two-thirds of the way full.

1. Heat the butter in a nonstick skillet. Add the onions and mushrooms and sauté until the onions are beginning to soften. Add half of the onion and mushroom mixture to a 4-quart slow cooker. Add the turkey. Sprinkle with sage, salt, and pepper. Top with the remaining onion and mushroom mixture.

2. Add the water. Cook on high for 2–3 hours or on low for 6–8 hours.

PER SERVING Calories: 150 | Fat: 1.5g | Sodium: 110mg | Carbohydrates: 3g | Fiber: <1g | Protein: 29g

Buffalo Chicken Sandwich Filling

Try this on crusty rolls and top with crumbled blue cheese or low-fat blue cheese dressing.

INGREDIENTS | SERVES 4

4 boneless, skinless chicken thighs

¼ cup diced onion

1 clove garlic, minced

½ teaspoon freshly ground black pepper

⅛ teaspoon salt

2 cups buffalo wing sauce

Lower-Fat Blue Cheese Dressing

In a small bowl stir 3 tablespoons reduced-fat blue cheese crumbles, 3 tablespoons fat-free buttermilk, ¼ cup reduced-fat mayonnaise, ½ tablespoon lemon juice, ⅛ teaspoon Worcestershire sauce, 1 pinch black pepper, and ½ tablespoon reduced-fat sour cream. Store in an airtight container for up to 3 days.

1. Place all ingredients in a 4-quart slow cooker. Stir. Cook on high for 2–3 hours or until the chicken is easily shredded with a fork. If the sauce is very thin, cook on high uncovered for 30 minutes or until thickened.

2. Shred the chicken and toss with the sauce.

PER SERVING Calories: 160 | Fat: 7g | Sodium: 3,470mg | Carbohydrates: 11g | Fiber: 1g | Protein: 14g

Sweet and Spicy Pulled Chicken

Make this recipe after breakfast and it will be ready by lunchtime.

INGREDIENTS | SERVES 4

1¾ pounds boneless, skinless chicken thighs
¼ cup chili sauce
¼ cup balsamic vinegar
2 tablespoons ginger preserves
2 tablespoons pineapple juice
2 tablespoons lime juice
1 teaspoon ground cayenne
½ teaspoon ground chipotle
½ teaspoon hot paprika
1 jalapeño, minced
3 cloves garlic, minced
1 teaspoon yellow hot sauce

1. Place all ingredients in a round 2- or 4-quart slow cooker. Cook on low for 3½ hours, or for 1½ hours on low and then turn it up to high for an additional hour.

2. When done, the meat should shred easily with a fork. Thoroughly shred the chicken. Toss to coat the meat evenly with the sauce.

PER SERVING Calories: 470 | Fat: 22g | Sodium: 440mg | Carbohydrates: 12g | Fiber: 1g | Protein: 52g

Tarragon Chicken

The tarragon infuses the chicken with flavor without added fat.

INGREDIENTS | SERVES 4

2 split chicken breasts
2 cups loosely packed fresh tarragon
1 onion, sliced
¼ teaspoon salt
¼ teaspoon freshly ground black pepper

1. Place the chicken in a 4-quart slow cooker. Top with remaining ingredients. Cook on low for 7–8 hours.

2. Remove the chicken from the slow cooker. Peel off the skin and discard. Discard the tarragon and onion.

PER SERVING Calories: 100 | Fat: 1.5g | Sodium: 190mg | Carbohydrates: 5g | Fiber: 0g | Protein: 15g

Chicken Piccata

Serve over mashed potatoes or egg noodles.

INGREDIENTS | SERVES 4

2 boneless, skinless thin-cut chicken breasts

1 cup flour

1 teaspoon canola oil

¼ cup lemon juice

3 tablespoons nonpareil capers

¾ cup Chicken Stock (page 17)

Dredge Details

Dredging is the process in which food is dragged through dry ingredients like flour or breadcrumbs to coat. Dredging can be a one-step process, but if a thicker crust or coating is desired, the food is dredged in flour once, dipped in egg, then dredged through flour, cornmeal, or breadcrumbs. In slow cooking, dredging often has a dual purpose of coating the meat and thickening the sauce.

1. Dredge both sides of the chicken breasts in the flour. Discard leftover flour.

2. Heat the oil in a nonstick pan. Quickly sear the chicken on each side.

3. Place the chicken, lemon juice, capers, and stock into a 4-quart slow cooker.

4. Cook on high for 3 hours or for 6 hours on low.

PER SERVING Calories: 220 | Fat: 3.5g | Sodium: 290mg | Carbohydrates: 27g | Fiber: 1g | Protein: 18g

Caribbean Chicken Curry

Traditional Jamaican curries are cooked for long periods of time over the stove top, making them a logical fit for the slow cooker. The spices meld together and the chicken is meltingly tender.

INGREDIENTS | SERVES 8

1 tablespoon Madras curry powder

1 teaspoon allspice

½ teaspoon ground cloves

½ teaspoon ground nutmeg

1 teaspoon ground ginger

2 pounds boneless, skinless chicken thighs, cubed

1 teaspoon canola oil

1 onion, chopped

2 cloves garlic, chopped

2 jalapeños, chopped

½ pound red skin potatoes, cubed

⅓ cup light coconut milk

1. In a medium bowl, whisk together the curry powder, allspice, cloves, nutmeg, and ginger. Add the chicken and toss to coat each piece evenly.

2. Place the chicken in a nonstick skillet and quickly sauté until the chicken starts to brown. Add to a 4-quart slow cooker along with the remaining spice mixture.

3. Heat the oil in a nonstick skillet and sauté the onions, garlic, and peppers until fragrant. Add to the slow cooker.

4. Add the potatoes and coconut milk to the slow cooker. Stir. Cook 7–8 hours on low.

PER SERVING Calories: 290 | Fat: 15g | Sodium: 105mg | Carbohydrates: 7g | Fiber: 1g | Protein: 30g

Chicken Braised in Beer

Serve this as-is or in any recipe that calls for cooked chicken.

INGREDIENTS | **SERVES 6**

3 boneless, skinless chicken breasts
1 onion, quartered
6 ounces beer
1½ cups water
2 cloves garlic

1. Place all ingredients in a 4-quart slow cooker. Cook on low for 6 hours.

2. Remove the chicken breasts and discard the cooking liquid.

PER SERVING Calories: 80 | Fat: 0.5g | Sodium: 40mg | Carbohydrates: 2g | Fiber: 0g | Protein: 14g

Thai-Influenced Braised Chicken Thighs

A flavorful poaching liquid ensures a flavorful chicken thigh. This sauce has aromatic galangal and ginger, both of which are used extensively in Thai cuisine.

INGREDIENTS | **SERVES 4**

4 boneless, skinless chicken thighs
3 tablespoons fish sauce
3 tablespoons soy sauce
3 tablespoons lime juice
1" knob galangal root, minced
1" knob ginger, minced
1 shallot, thinly sliced
2 cloves garlic, thinly sliced
¼ teaspoon white pepper

Place all ingredients into a 4-quart slow cooker. Cook on high for 2½ hours. Discard the cooking liquid before serving.

PER SERVING Calories: 170 | Fat: 6g | Sodium: 1,840mg | Carbohydrates: 13g | Fiber: 0g | Protein: 18g

Chicken Makhani

Chicken Makhani is commonly known as Butter Chicken. Butter Chicken is a bit of a misnomer as the dish traditionally includes only a tablespoon or so of butter.

INGREDIENTS | SERVES 4

1 pound boneless, skinless chicken breasts or thighs

2 shallots, minced

2 cloves garlic, minced

½" knob ginger, minced

2 tablespoons lemon juice

2 teaspoons garam masala

1 teaspoon ground cumin

½ teaspoon cayenne

½ teaspoon ground cloves

½ teaspoon fenugreek

¼ teaspoon salt

½ teaspoon freshly ground black pepper

1 tablespoon butter

1 tablespoon tomato paste

¾ cup fat-free Greek yogurt

1. Place the chicken, shallots, garlic, ginger, lemon juice, the spices, butter, and tomato paste into a 4-quart slow cooker. Stir. Cook on low for 5 hours.

2. Stir in the yogurt. Serve immediately.

PER SERVING Calories: 330 | Fat: 7g | Sodium: 310mg | Carbohydrates: 27g | Fiber: <1g | Protein: 42g

Do-It-Yourself Greek Yogurt

Greek yogurt is super-thick and creamy but low in fat. It is available in many grocery stores but can be tricky to find in some areas. A reasonable facsimile can be made by lining a colander with cheesecloth and straining low-fat regular yogurt overnight. Be sure to start with twice as much yogurt as the final product should be because the yogurt will reduce by half.

Moroccan Chicken

This dish was inspired by traditional North African tagines and adapted for the slow cooker.

INGREDIENTS | SERVES 6

½ teaspoon coriander

½ teaspoon cinnamon

¼ teaspoon salt

1 teaspoon cumin

4 boneless, skinless chicken thighs, diced

½ cup water

4 cloves garlic, minced

1 onion, thinly sliced

1" knob ginger, minced

15 ounces canned chickpeas, drained and rinsed

4 ounces dried apricots, halved

1. Place all of the spices, chicken, water, garlic, onion, and ginger into a 4-quart slow cooker. Cook on low for 5 hours.

2. Stir in the chickpeas and apricots and cook on high for 40 minutes.

PER SERVING Calories: 210 | Fat: 4.5g | Sodium: 340mg | Carbohydrates: 30g | Fiber: 5g | Protein: 13g

Ginger Caramelized Chicken

In this Thai-influenced dish, the chicken is slightly sweet and very fragrant.
Look for caramel syrup in Asian grocery stores. It is not a dessert item.

INGREDIENTS | SERVES 4

1 pound boneless, skinless chicken breasts

1 teaspoon canola oil

2 cloves garlic, minced

2 tablespoons minced fresh ginger

2 Thai bird peppers, minced

1 shallot, minced

2 tablespoons fish sauce

1 tablespoon caramel syrup

¼ cup Chicken Stock (page 17)

1. Cut the chicken breasts into 1"-wide strips. Heat the oil in a nonstick skillet. Add the chicken, garlic, ginger, peppers, and shallot. Sauté until the onions and garlic are fragrant.

2. Add the mixture to a 4-quart slow cooker. Add the remaining ingredients, and stir. Cook for 4–5 hours on low.

PER SERVING Calories: 270 | Fat: 5g | Sodium: 810mg | Carbohydrates: 15g | Fiber: 0g | Protein: 38g

Homemade Caramel Syrup

Place ⅔ cup sugar and ¼ cup water in a large, heavy-bottomed saucepan. Bring to a boil and continue to boil for 10–15 minutes. When the caramel reaches 180°F, remove it from the heat and allow it to cool to room temperature. Store refrigerated in an airtight container.

Mango Duck Breast

Slow-cooked mangoes soften and create their own sauce in this easy duck dish.

INGREDIENTS | SERVES 4

2 boneless, skinless duck breasts

1 large mango, cubed

¼ cup duck stock or Chicken Stock (page 17)

1 tablespoon ginger juice

1 tablespoon minced hot pepper

1 tablespoon minced shallot

Place all ingredients into a 4-quart slow cooker. Cook on low for 4 hours.

PER SERVING Calories: 150 | Fat: 4g | Sodium: 70mg | Carbohydrates: 10g | Fiber: 1g | Protein: 17g

Tuscan Chicken

This simple dish is perfect served over warm white beans.

INGREDIENTS | SERVES 4

1 pound boneless, skinless chicken breast tenderloins

4 cloves garlic, minced

1 shallot, minced

2 tablespoons white wine vinegar

1 tablespoon lemon juice

1 tablespoon minced fresh rosemary

1 cup Chicken Stock (page 17)

Place all ingredients into a 4-quart slow cooker. Stir. Cook on low for 4 hours or until the chicken is fully cooked.

PER SERVING Calories: 230 | Fat: 5g | Sodium: 170mg | Carbohydrates: 7g | Fiber: 0g | Protein: 37g

Chicken with Figs

This recipe was inspired by traditional Moroccan tangines, a type of savory slow-cooked stew. Try it with whole-grain couscous or quinoa.

INGREDIENTS | SERVES 8

½ pound boneless, skinless chicken thighs

¾ pound boneless, skinless chicken breasts

¾ cup dried figs

1 sweet potato, peeled and diced

1 onion, chopped

3 cloves garlic, minced

2 teaspoons cumin

1 teaspoon coriander

½ teaspoon cayenne pepper

½ teaspoon ground ginger

½ teaspoon turmeric

½ teaspoon ground orange peel

½ teaspoon freshly ground black pepper

2¾ cups Chicken Stock (page 17)

¼ cup orange juice

1. Cube the chicken. Quickly sauté the chicken in a dry nonstick skillet until it starts to turn white. Drain off any excess grease.

2. Place the chicken and remaining ingredients into a 4-quart slow cooker. Stir. Cook for 6 hours on low. Stir before serving.

PER SERVING Calories: 230 | Fat: 6g | Sodium: 180mg | Carbohydrates: 22g | Fiber: 3g | Protein: 24g

Turkey Joes

This not-so-sloppy version of the cafeteria classic is perfect served on whole-grain rolls and topped with a sprinkle of sharp Cheddar.

INGREDIENTS | SERVES 4

1½ pounds ground turkey breast

6 ounces tomato paste

½ cup water

4 cloves garlic, minced

1 onion, minced

1 carrot, minced

1 teaspoon ground chipotle chile

1 teaspoon smoked paprika

1 teaspoon cayenne pepper

1 teaspoon cumin

½ teaspoon cinnamon

¼ teaspoon allspice

⅛ teaspoon cloves

⅛ teaspoon salt

1. In a nonstick skillet, sauté the turkey until cooked through, breaking up any large chunks. Drain off any excess fat. Add to a 4-quart slow cooker.

2. Add the remaining ingredients. Stir to distribute the spices evenly. Cook on low up to 8 hours. Stir prior to serving.

PER SERVING Calories: 320 | Fat: 15g | Sodium: 580mg | Carbohydrates: 14g | Fiber: 4g | Protein: 32g

Cooking with Ground Turkey

Ground turkey breast is 98% fat free, and each serving has 26 grams of protein. Due to its low-fat content, it is important to add some liquid so it does not dry out. Turkey or chicken broth and sauces or water can be added to turkey to keep it moist.

Peruvian Chicken with Aji Verde

Juicy chicken breasts are the perfect foil for this light, creamy cilantro-spiked sauce. Aji Verde is often served as a dipping sauce, but in this dish it seeps into the chicken, infusing it with flavor.

INGREDIENTS | SERVES 4

5 cloves garlic, mashed

2 bone-in chicken breasts

2 tablespoons red wine vinegar

1 teaspoon cumin

1 teaspoon sugar

2 tablespoons soy sauce

2 jalapeños, chopped

½ cup cilantro

⅓ cup water

⅓ cup Cotija cheese

1 teaspoon apple cider vinegar

¼ teaspoon salt

1. Spread the cloves of garlic over the chicken pieces. Place into an oval 4-quart slow cooker. Pour the vinegar, cumin, sugar, and soy sauce over the chicken. Cook on low for 5 hours or until the chicken is thoroughly cooked.

2. In a food processor, pulse together the jalapeños, cilantro, water, cheese, cider vinegar, and salt.

3. Remove the chicken from the slow cooker. Remove and discard the skin. Spread the sauce on each breast. Return to the slow cooker and cook on low 15 minutes before serving.

PER SERVING Calories: 230 | Fat: 16g | Sodium: 800mg | Carbohydrates: 4g | Fiber: <1g | Protein: 19g

¿Qué es el Queso Cotija?

Cotija cheese is a Mexican cheese made from cow's milk. It can be found in large blocks or grated. It has a flavor profile similar to Parmesan and can be rather crumbly. Use it as a topping for salads, tacos, soups, beans, or tostadas.

Thai Peanut Chicken

*In this healthy version of the takeout favorite, the broccoli
is steamed in the broth as the chicken slow cooks.*

INGREDIENTS | SERVES 6

1 pound boneless, skinless chicken breasts, cubed

2 cups broccoli florets

1 cup Chicken Stock (page 17)

¼ cup coarsely chopped peanuts

3 tablespoons soy sauce

2 tablespoons minced Thai bird peppers

2 tablespoons minced garlic

2 tablespoons minced fresh ginger

¼ cup diced green onions

1. Place the chicken, broccoli, stock, peanuts, soy sauce, pepper, garlic, and ginger into a 4-quart slow cooker. Stir.

2. Cook on low for 4–5 hours or until the chicken is thoroughly cooked. Stir in the green onions prior to serving.

PER SERVING Calories: 210 | Fat: 7g | Sodium: 620mg | Carbohydrates: 6g | Fiber: 2g | Protein: 28g

Wild Rice–Stuffed Turkey Breast Cutlets

All this hearty dish needs is a side of steamed vegetables to make it a complete meal.

INGREDIENTS | SERVES 4

1 onion, sliced

4 ounces button mushrooms, minced

1 cup cooked wild rice

4 turkey breast cutlets (about 1 pound)

½ cup Chicken Stock (page 17)

1. Place the onions and mushrooms on the bottom of a 4-quart slow cooker.

2. Divide the wild rice into four portions. Place a single portion in the center of each cutlet. Roll, rice-side in, and secure with a toothpick or kitchen twine. Place on top of the onions and mushrooms. Pour the broth over top.

3. Cook on low for 4 hours.

PER SERVING Calories: 190 | Fat: 1g | Sodium: 150mg | Carbohydrates: 12g | Fiber: 1g | Protein: 31g

Chicken Fricassee

Chicken Fricassee is a dish that is easily adapted for personal taste.
Fennel, mushrooms, or parsnips can be used with great success.

INGREDIENTS | SERVES 6

2 cups sliced red cabbage

2 carrots, cut into coin-sized pieces

2 stalks celery, diced

1 onion, sliced

3 bone-in chicken breasts

¾ cup Chicken Stock (page 17)

2 teaspoons paprika

2 teaspoons dried thyme

2 teaspoons dried parsley

1. Place the cabbage, carrots, celery, and onions on the bottom of an oval 4-quart slow cooker.

2. Place the chicken skin-side up on top of the vegetables. Pour the stock over the chicken and sprinkle it evenly with the spices. Pat the spices onto the chicken skin.

3. Cook on low 6 hours or until the chicken is cooked through. Remove the skin prior to serving.

PER SERVING Calories: 170 | Fat: 7g | Sodium: 130mg | Carbohydrates: 9g | Fiber: 2g | Protein: 17g

Chicken Saltimbocca

Saltimbocca can refer to a number of ham or prosciutto-wrapped meat dishes. In this version, the mild chicken takes on the strong flavors of the capers and prosciutto.

INGREDIENTS | SERVES 4

4 boneless, skinless breast tenderloins

4 paper-thin slices prosciutto

1½ cups Chicken Broth (page 17)

3 tablespoons capote capers

¼ cup minced fresh sage

1. Wrap each tenderloin in prosciutto. Secure with a toothpick if necessary. Place them in a single layer in an oval 4-quart slow cooker.

2. Pour the broth over the chicken. Sprinkle with the capers and sage. Cook on low for 5 hours or until the chicken is fully cooked. Discard the cooking liquid prior to serving.

PER SERVING Calories: 150 | Fat: 9g | Sodium: 620mg | Carbohydrates: 9g | Fiber: <1g | Protein: 9g

Balsamic Chicken and Spinach

Serve this with rice pilaf.

INGREDIENTS | SERVES 4

¾ pound boneless, skinless chicken breasts, cut into strips

¼ cup balsamic vinegar

4 cloves garlic, minced

1 tablespoon minced fresh oregano

1 tablespoon minced fresh Italian parsley

½ teaspoon freshly ground black pepper

5 ounces baby spinach

1. Place the chicken, vinegar, garlic, and spices into a 4-quart slow cooker. Stir. Cook on low for 6 hours.

2. Stir in the baby spinach and continue to cook until it starts to wilt, about 15 minutes. Stir before serving.

PER SERVING Calories: 180 | Fat: 3g | Sodium: 125mg | Carbohydrates: 10g | Fiber: 2g | Protein: 28g

Turkey Bratwurst with Peppers and Onions

Cubanelle peppers have a bright, peppery flavor that is a welcome change from the ubiquitous bell pepper.

INGREDIENTS | **SERVES 4**

4 turkey bratwursts
3 cubanelle peppers
2 onions, thinly sliced
¼ teaspoon salt
½ teaspoon freshly ground black pepper
2 tablespoons water

1. Prick each bratwurst once with a fork. Quickly brown them on all sides in a dry nonstick skillet. Cut off the tops of each pepper and remove the seeds and stem. Slice into thin strips, vertically.

2. Place half of the onions and peppers on the bottom of a 4-quart slow cooker. Place the bratwurst on top of the onions and peppers. Top with the remaining pepper and onions. Sprinkle with salt, pepper, and water. Cook on low for 6 hours.

PER SERVING Calories: 160 | Fat: 8g | Sodium: 200mg | Carbohydrates: 8g | Fiber: 2g | Protein: 15g

Spicy Roasted Turkey Breast

This turkey breast is wonderful as a main dish, but it is also delightful in a spicy turkey salad.

INGREDIENTS | **SERVES 6**

2 teaspoons cayenne pepper

2 teaspoons chipotle pepper

2 teaspoons freshly ground black pepper

½ teaspoon salt

2½ pounds bone-in turkey breast

2 jalapeños, minced

1 teaspoon hot sauce

¾ cup water

1. Rub the dry spices into the turkey breast. Place into an oval 4-quart slow cooker. Top with jalapeños, hot sauce, and water.

2. Cook on low for 8 hours or until fully cooked. Remove the skin before serving.

PER SERVING Calories: 300 | Fat: 14g | Sodium: 330mg | Carbohydrates: 1g | Fiber: <1g | Protein: 42g

Canned Good Safety

Most canned goods are stamped with a "use by" date. If not, plan on eating the food within 18 months of purchase. Discard any cans that have rusted, are bulging, or are dented. That can be a sign that the integrity of the seal has been broken or the food inside has spoiled.

Vegetarian

Fresh Chile Grits

Grits are most often served at breakfast, but they make a great side dish as well.

INGREDIENTS | SERVES 10

1 tablespoon canola oil

1 medium onion, diced

2 cloves garlic, minced

4¼ cups Roasted Vegetable Stock (page 19)

1½ cups stone-ground grits

4 jalapeños, sliced

1 teaspoon dried thyme

½ teaspoon ground black pepper

¼ teaspoon salt

¼ cup shredded reduced-fat sharp Cheddar

1. Heat the canola oil in a small skillet. Add the onion and garlic and sauté until softened.

2. Add the onion, garlic, stock, grits, jalapeños, and spices to a 4-quart slow cooker. Stir. Cook on low for 8 hours. Stir the cheese into the grits before serving.

PER SERVING Calories: 120 | Fat: 2.5g | Sodium: 180mg | Carbohydrates: 21g | Fiber: <1g | Protein: 3g

The Nitty Gritty

Grits are coarsely ground pieces of corn simmered with water or broth until they are thick and creamy. Yellow grits are made from the whole kernel, while white grits are made from hulled kernels. Either variety can be used in this recipe.

Spiced "Baked" Eggplant

Serve this as a main dish over rice or as a side dish as-is.

INGREDIENTS | SERVES 4

1 pound cubed eggplant
⅓ cup sliced onion
½ teaspoon red pepper flakes
½ teaspoon crushed rosemary
¼ cup lemon juice

Place all ingredients in a 1½–2-quart slow cooker. Cook on low for 3 hours or until the eggplant is tender.

PER SERVING Calories: 40 | Fat: 0g | Sodium: 0mg | Carbohydrates: 9g | Fiber: 4g | Protein: 1g

Cold Snap

Take care not to put a cold ceramic slow cooker insert directly into the slow cooker. The sudden shift in temperature can cause it to crack. If you want to prepare your ingredients the night before use, refrigerate them in reusable containers, not in the insert.

Wild Mushroom Risotto

This makes a great side dish, or try it as a main course paired with a green salad.

INGREDIENTS | SERVES 6

1 teaspoon olive oil
1 shallot, minced
2 cloves garlic, minced
8 ounces sliced assorted wild mushrooms
2 cups Roasted Vegetable Stock (page 19)
2 cups Arborio rice
3 cups water

1. Heat the oil in a nonstick pan. Sauté the shallot, garlic, and mushrooms until soft. Add ½ cup stock and cook until half of the stock has evaporated. Add the rice and cook until the liquid is fully absorbed.

2. Scrape the rice mixture into a 4-quart slow cooker. Add the water and remaining stock, and cook on low for 1 hour. Stir before serving.

PER SERVING Calories: 150 | Fat: 1g | Sodium: 95mg | Carbohydrates: 33g | Fiber: <1g | Protein: 5g

Eggplant "Lasagna"

This no-noodle dish makes for a hearty vegetarian meal. Serve it with a side salad.

INGREDIENTS | SERVES 8

2 1-pound eggplants

1 tablespoon kosher salt

30 ounces skim-milk ricotta

2 teaspoons olive oil, divided use

1 medium onion, diced

3 cloves garlic, minced

1 tablespoon minced Italian parsley

1 tablespoon minced basil

28 ounces canned crushed tomatoes

1 shallot, diced

4 ounces fresh spinach

1 tablespoon dried mixed Italian seasoning

¼ teaspoon salt

½ teaspoon freshly ground black pepper

Do-It-Yourself Italian Herb Mix

While most spice companies make an Italian mix of dried herbs, it is easy to make your own. Mix 1 teaspoon each of oregano, basil, marjoram, thyme, savory, and crushed rosemary. Store in an airtight container.

1. Slice the eggplant lengthwise into ¼"-thick slices. Place in a bowl or colander and sprinkle with the salt. Allow it to sit for 15 minutes. Drain off the liquid. Rinse off the salt. Pat dry. Set aside. Line a colander with cheesecloth or paper towels. Pour the ricotta into the colander and drain for 15 minutes.

2. Heat 1 teaspoon olive oil in a nonstick pan. Sauté the onion and garlic until just softened. Add the parsley, basil, and crushed tomatoes. Sauté until the sauce thickens and the liquid has evaporated.

3. In a second nonstick pan, heat the remaining oil. Sauté the shallot and spinach until the spinach has wilted. Drain off any extra liquid. Stir this mixture and the Italian seasoning, salt, and pepper into the ricotta mixture. Set aside.

4. Preheat the oven to 375°F. Place the eggplant slices on baking sheets. Bake for 10 minutes. Cool slightly.

5. Pour one-third of the sauce onto the bottom of a 4-quart slow cooker. Top with a single layer of eggplant. Top with half of the cheese mixture. Add one-third of the sauce. Top with the rest of the cheese mixture. Layer the remaining eggplant on top, and then top with remaining sauce. Cook for 4 hours on low, then 30 minutes on high uncovered.

PER SERVING Calories: 240 | Fat: 10g | Sodium: 1,250mg | Carbohydrates: 23g | Fiber: 6g | Protein: 16g

Curried Lentils

Serve this Indian-style dish with hot rice.

INGREDIENTS | SERVES 6

2 teaspoons butter or canola oil

1 large onion, thinly sliced

2 cloves garlic, minced

2 jalapeños, diced

½ teaspoon red pepper flakes

½ teaspoon ground cumin

1 pound yellow lentils

6 cups water

½ teaspoon salt

½ teaspoon ground turmeric

4 cups chopped fresh spinach

1. Heat the butter or oil in a nonstick pan. Sauté the onion slices until they start to brown, about 8–10 minutes. Add the garlic, jalapeños, red pepper flakes, and cumin. Sauté for 2–3 minutes.

2. Add the onion mixture to a 4-quart slow cooker. Sort through the lentils and discard any rocks or foreign matter. Add the lentils to the slow cooker. Stir in the water, salt, and turmeric.

3. Cook on high for 2½ hours. Add the spinach. Stir and cook on high for an additional 15 minutes.

PER SERVING Calories: 280 | Fat: 2g | Sodium: 210mg | Carbohydrates: 49g | Fiber: 10g | Protein: 21g

Zucchini Ragout

A ragout is either a main-dish stew or a sauce. This one can be served as either.

INGREDIENTS | SERVES 6

5 ounces fresh spinach
3 zucchini, diced
½ cup diced red onion
2 stalks celery, diced
2 carrots, diced
1 parsnip, diced
3 tablespoons tomato paste
¼ cup water
1 teaspoon freshly ground black pepper
¼ teaspoon kosher salt
1 tablespoon minced basil
1 tablespoon minced Italian parsley
1 tablespoon minced oregano

Place all ingredients into a 4-quart slow cooker. Stir. Cook on low for 4 hours. Stir before serving.

PER SERVING Calories: 70 | Fat: 0g | Sodium: 220mg | Carbohydrates: 15g | Fiber: 4g | Protein: 3g

Portobello Barley

This method of cooking barley makes it as creamy as risotto but with the bonus of being high in fiber.

INGREDIENTS | SERVES 8

1 teaspoon olive oil
2 shallots, minced
2 cloves garlic, minced
3 Portobello mushroom caps, sliced
1 cup pearl barley
3¼ cups water
¼ teaspoon salt
½ teaspoon freshly ground black pepper
1 teaspoon crushed rosemary
1 teaspoon dried chervil
¼ cup grated Parmesan

1. Heat the oil in a nonstick skillet. Sauté the shallots, garlic, and mushrooms until softened.

2. Place the mushroom mixture into a 4-quart slow cooker. Add the barley, water, salt, pepper, rosemary, and chervil. Stir. Cook on low for 8–9 hours or on high for 4 hours.

3. Turn off the slow cooker and stir in the Parmesan. Serve immediately.

PER SERVING Calories: 130 | Fat: 1.5g | Sodium: 120mg | Carbohydrates: 25g | Fiber: 5g | Protein: 5g

Spring Vegetables Pasta Sauce

Make this sauce at the first hint of spring.

INGREDIENTS | **SERVES 4**

1 1-pound eggplant, cubed

2 zucchini, cubed

1 onion, minced

3 cloves garlic, minced

1 carrot, diced

28 ounces crushed tomatoes

1 tablespoon tomato paste

1 tablespoon minced fresh basil

½ teaspoon freshly ground black pepper

Place all ingredients into a 4-quart slow cooker and stir. Cook on low for 8–10 hours. Stir before serving.

PER SERVING Calories: 130 | Fat: 1g | Sodium: 320mg | Carbohydrates: 30g | Fiber: 10g | Protein: 6g

Cauliflower Chowder

In this rich chowder, puréed cauliflower takes the place of heavy cream.

INGREDIENTS | **SERVES 6**

2 pounds cauliflower florets

2 quarts Roasted Vegetable Stock (page 19) or water

1 onion, chopped

3 cloves garlic, minced

1 teaspoon white pepper

¼ teaspoon salt

1½ cups broccoli florets

2 carrots, cut into coins

1 stalk celery, diced

1. Place the cauliflower, stock, onions, garlic, pepper, and salt into a 4-quart slow cooker. Stir. Cook on low for 6 hours or until the cauliflower is fork tender.

2. Use an immersion blender to purée the cauliflower in the slow cooker until very smooth. Add the broccoli, carrots, and celery. Cook for 30 minutes or until the vegetables are fork-tender.

PER SERVING Calories: 90 | Fat: 1g | Sodium: 540mg | Carbohydrates: 16g | Fiber: 6g | Protein: 6g

Ratatouille

Ratatouille made in the slow cooker comes out surprisingly crisp-tender.

INGREDIENTS | **SERVES 4**

1 onion, roughly chopped

1 eggplant, sliced horizontally

2 zucchini, sliced

1 cubanelle pepper, sliced

3 tomatoes, cut into wedges

2 tablespoons minced fresh basil

2 tablespoons minced fresh Italian parsley

¼ teaspoon salt

½ teaspoon freshly ground black pepper

3 ounces tomato paste

¼ cup water

1. Place the onion, eggplant, zucchini, pepper, and tomatoes into a 4-quart slow cooker. Sprinkle with basil, parsley, salt, and pepper.

2. Whisk the tomato paste and water in a small bowl. Pour the mixture over the vegetables. Stir.

3. Cook on low for 4 hours or until the eggplant and zucchini are fork-tender.

PER SERVING Calories: 110 | Fat: 1g | Sodium: 330mg | Carbohydrates: 24g | Fiber: 8g | Protein: 5g

Thai Coconut Curry

Try this easy vegetarian curry tossed with rice noodles or over brown rice.

INGREDIENTS | SERVES 6

12 ounces extra-firm tofu

¼ cup unsweetened shredded coconut

¼ cup water

4 cloves garlic, minced

1 tablespoon minced fresh ginger

1 tablespoon minced galangal root

½ cup chopped onion

1 cup peeled and diced sweet potato

1 cup broccoli florets

1 cup snow peas

3 tablespoons tamari

1 tablespoon vegetarian fish sauce

1 tablespoon chili-garlic sauce

½ cup minced cilantro

½ cup light coconut milk

1. Slice the tofu into ½"-thick triangles. Place into a 4-quart slow cooker. Top with coconut, water, garlic, ginger, galangal, onion, sweet potato, broccoli, snow peas, tamari, vegetarian fish sauce, and chili-garlic sauce. Stir to distribute all ingredients evenly. Cook on low for 5 hours.

2. Stir in the cilantro and coconut milk. Cook on low for an additional 20 minutes. Stir prior to serving.

PER SERVING Calories: 140 | Fat: 8g | Sodium: 870mg | Carbohydrates: 13g | Fiber: 3g | Protein: 7g

Vegetable Stew with Dumplings

*The cornmeal dumplings perfectly complement the fall vegetables in
this hearty stew, making it a complete meal in one pot.*

INGREDIENTS | SERVES 6

1 teaspoon olive oil

3 russet potatoes, peeled and diced

3 carrots, cut into ½" chunks

2 stalks celery, diced

1 onion, diced

1 rutabaga, diced

1 cup diced celeriac

1 cup cauliflower florets

2 quarts Roasted Vegetable Stock
(page 19)

1 tablespoon fresh thyme

1 tablespoon fresh parsley

⅔ cup water

2 tablespoons canola oil

½ cup cornmeal

2 teaspoons baking powder

½ teaspoon salt

1. Heat the olive oil in a nonstick skillet. Add all of the vegetables. Sauté until the onions are soft and translucent. Add to a 4-quart slow cooker.

2. Add the stock, thyme, and parsley. Stir. Cook for 6 hours or until the vegetables are fork tender. Stir.

3. In a medium bowl, stir the water, oil, cornmeal, baking powder, and salt. Drop in ¼-cup mounds in a single layer on top of the stew. Cover and cook on high for 20 minutes without lifting the lid. The dumplings will look fluffy and light when fully cooked.

PER SERVING Calories: 270 | Fat: 7g | Sodium: 810mg | Carbohydrates: 46g | Fiber: 7g | Protein: 6g

Eggplant Caponata

Serve this on small slices of Italian bread as an appetizer or use as a filling in sandwiches or wraps.

INGREDIENTS | SERVES 8

2 1-pound eggplants
1 teaspoon olive oil
1 red onion, diced
4 cloves garlic, minced
1 stalk celery, diced
2 tomatoes, diced
2 tablespoons nonpareil capers
2 tablespoons toasted pine nuts
1 teaspoon red pepper flakes
¼ cup red wine vinegar

1. Pierce the eggplants with a fork. Cook on high in a 4- or 6-quart slow cooker for 2 hours.

2. Allow to cool. Peel off the skin. Slice each in half and remove the seeds. Discard the skin and seeds.

3. Place the pulp in a food processor. Pulse until smooth. Set aside.

4. Heat the oil in a nonstick skillet. Sauté the onion, garlic, and celery until the onion is soft. Add the eggplant and tomatoes. Sauté 3 minutes.

5. Return to the slow cooker and add the capers, pine nuts, red pepper flakes, and vinegar. Stir. Cook on low 30 minutes. Stir prior to serving.

PER SERVING Calories: 70 | Fat: 2.5g | Sodium: 75mg | Carbohydrates: 11g | Fiber: 5g | Protein: 2g

Gumbo z'Herbs

This might not be what springs to mind when thinking about gumbo, but it is actually quite popular in New Orleans, especially on Good Friday when many abstain from eating meat. Serve over rice with a sprinkle of filé powder on top.

INGREDIENTS | SERVES 8

1 bunch mustard greens

1 bunch turnip greens

1 bunch beet greens

1 bunch spinach

1 teaspoon canola oil

2 onions, diced

6 cloves garlic, minced

2 stalks celery (including greens), diced

2 bell peppers, chopped

1 bunch dandelion greens, chopped

1 bunch watercress, chopped

1 bunch carrot tops, chopped

1½ cups shredded cabbage

1½ cups chopped butter lettuce

2 large turnips, diced

1 cup diced green onions

3½ quarts Roasted Vegetable Stock (page 19) or water

1 tablespoon hickory liquid smoke

1 tablespoon minced fresh thyme

1 teaspoon crushed red pepper flakes

½ teaspoon freshly ground black pepper

½ teaspoon cloves

½ teaspoon allspice

¼ teaspoon salt

1. Tear the mustard greens, turnip greens, beet greens, and spinach into bite-sized pieces. Discard the ribs. Thoroughly clean the greens of any grit.

2. Heat the oil in a large pot. Add the onions, garlic, celery, and peppers, and sauté 3 minutes. Add all of the greens and stir until the greens start to wilt. Add to a 4- to 6-quart slow cooker.

3. Add the remaining ingredients to the slow cooker. Stir. Cook on low for 6 hours. Stir prior to serving.

PER SERVING Calories: 140 | Fat: 2.5g | Sodium: 810mg | Carbohydrates: 27g | Fiber: 11g | Protein: 9g

How to Wash and Prepare Greens

Greens are notoriously dirty, but they are not terribly difficult to clean. Remove the leaves from the ribs. Tear the leaves into bite-sized pieces. Discard the ribs. Plunge the greens into a large bowl of cold water and swish them around. Drain the water and repeat. Use a salad spinner to dry out the greens. If there is any grit at the bottom of the spinner after spinning, rinse them again. Spin until dry.

Chickpea Curry

This slow cooker version of chole, a traditional Indian curry, is very low in fat but high in fiber and flavor.

INGREDIENTS | SERVES 8

1 cup dried chickpeas

Water, as needed

1 teaspoon olive oil

1 onion, diced

3 cloves garlic, minced

1 tablespoon minced fresh ginger

1 large tomato, diced

2 tablespoons tomato paste

1 tablespoon cumin

1 teaspoon turmeric

1 teaspoon coriander

1 teaspoon asafetida powder

1 teaspoon cayenne

¼ teaspoon cinnamon

1. Place the chickpeas into a 4-quart slow cooker. Fill the rest of the insert with water. Allow the chickpeas to soak overnight. Drain and return to the slow cooker.

2. Heat the oil in a nonstick pan. Sauté the onions, garlic, and ginger until the onions are soft and translucent. Add to the slow cooker.

3. Add the remaining ingredients. Stir. Cook on low for 8–10 hours. Stir before serving.

PER SERVING Calories: 110 | Fat: 2g | Sodium: 40mg | Carbohydrates: 19g | Fiber: 4g | Protein: 6g

Quick Raita

In a small bowl, stir ½ grated English cucumber, 1 cup fat-free Greek yogurt, ¼ cup minced fresh mint, ½ teaspoon cumin, and ¼ teaspoon cayenne. Refrigerate for 2 hours. Serve cold as a condiment with Indian curries to cut the heat.

Sweet and Sour Tofu

This recipe is not only kid-friendly but vegan and gluten-free.
Serve it over rice and garnish with diced green onions.

INGREDIENTS | SERVES 6

12 ounces extra-firm tofu, cubed
¼ cup rice vinegar
3 tablespoons water
1 tablespoon sesame seeds
1 tablespoon brown sugar
1 tablespoon tamari
1 tablespoon pineapple juice
1 teaspoon ground ginger
¾ cup pineapple chunks
1 cup snow peas
½ cup sliced onion

1. Spray a nonstick skillet with cooking spray. Sauté the tofu until it is lightly browned on each side. Add to a 4-quart slow cooker.

2. In a small bowl, whisk together the vinegar, water, sesame seeds, brown sugar, tamari, pineapple juice, and ginger until the sugar fully dissolves. Pour over the tofu.

3. Add the remaining ingredients. Cook on low for 4 hours. Remove the lid and cook on low for 30 minutes.

PER SERVING Calories: 80 | Fat: 2g | Sodium: 210mg | Carbohydrates: 10g | Fiber: 1g | Protein: 5g

Herb-Stuffed Tomatoes

Serve these Italian-influenced stuffed tomatoes with a simple salad for an easy, light meal.

INGREDIENTS | SERVES 4

4 large tomatoes

1 cup cooked quinoa

1 stalk celery, minced

1 tablespoon minced fresh garlic

2 tablespoons minced fresh oregano

2 tablespoons minced fresh Italian parsley

1 teaspoon dried chervil

1 teaspoon fennel seeds

¾ cup water

1. Cut out the core of each tomato and discard. Scoop out the seeds, leaving the walls of the tomato intact.

2. In a small bowl, stir together the quinoa, celery, garlic, and spices. Divide evenly among the four tomatoes.

3. Place the filled tomatoes in a single layer in an oval 4-quart slow cooker. Pour the water into the bottom of the slow cooker. Cook on low for 4 hours.

PER SERVING Calories: 210 | Fat: 3.5g | Sodium: 30mg | Carbohydrates: 39g | Fiber: 5g | Protein: 8g

CHAPTER 12

Vegan

"Roasted" Beets

Slice and eat as a side dish or use in any recipe that calls for cooked beets.

INGREDIENTS | SERVES 8

2 pounds whole beets, stems and leaves removed

2 tablespoons lemon juice

¼ cup balsamic vinegar

Easy Pickled Beets

Slice 1 pound roasted beets. Place in a small saucepan and add ½ cup sugar, ½ cup white distilled vinegar, ¼ teaspoon cinnamon, and ½ small onion, sliced. Bring to a boil. Cool, and store in an airtight container overnight before serving.

1. Place the beets in the bottom of a 4-quart slow cooker. Pour the lemon juice and vinegar over the top. Cook for 2 hours on low or until they are easily pierced with a fork.

2. Remove from the slow cooker. Allow to cool slightly. Wrap a beet in a paper towel and rub it to remove the skin. Repeat for the remaining beets.

PER SERVING Calories: 60 | Fat: 0g | Sodium: 90mg | Carbohydrates: 14g | Fiber: 3g | Protein: 2g

Soy Almonds

These slightly spicy almonds are a wonderful alternative to plain or sweetened almonds. Try them in a salad.

INGREDIENTS | SERVES 15

2 cups whole almonds

2 tablespoons low-sodium soy sauce or tamari

½ teaspoon sesame oil

1 teaspoon Chinese five-spice powder

1. Place all ingredients into a 4-quart oval slow cooker. Stir.

2. Cook for 15 minutes on high, uncovered. Reduce heat to low and continue to cook, uncovered, for 1 hour on low, stirring occasionally, or until the almonds are dry.

PER SERVING Calories: 110 | Fat: 10g | Sodium: 50mg | Carbohydrates: 4g | Fiber: 2g | Protein: 4g

Blackberry Jam

This easy low-sugar jam does not need to be canned; it will keep up to a month in the refrigerator.

INGREDIENTS | **SERVES 20**

3 cups fresh blackberries
1¾ ounces low-sugar / no-sugar pectin
½ cup sugar
¾ cup water

1. Place all ingredients in a 2-quart slow cooker. Stir.

2. Cook on high, uncovered, for 5 hours. Pour into an airtight container.

3. Refrigerate overnight before using.

PER SERVING Calories: 35 | Fat: 0g | Sodium: 5mg | Carbohydrates: 9g | Fiber: 1g | Protein: 0g

Marinara Sauce

This classic sauce is delicious over spaghetti or in Lasagna with Spinach (page 225)

INGREDIENTS | **SERVES 8**

1 tablespoon olive oil
1 large onion, diced
2 cloves garlic, minced
1 tablespoon minced fresh basil
1 tablespoon minced fresh Italian parsley
1 stalk celery, diced
28 ounces canned whole tomatoes in purée
28 ounces canned crushed tomatoes
15 ounces diced tomatoes in juice

1. Heat the olive oil in a medium nonstick skillet. Sauté the onions and garlic until the onion is soft, about 3 minutes.

2. Add the onions and garlic to a 6-quart slow cooker. Add the herbs, celery, and tomatoes. Stir to distribute the spices. Cook on low for 10–12 hours.

PER SERVING Calories: 90 | Fat: 2g | Sodium: 290mg | Carbohydrates: 16g | Fiber: 4g | Protein: 3g

White Bean Cassoulet

The longer you cook this cassoulet, the creamier it gets.

INGREDIENTS | **SERVES 8**

1 pound dried cannellini beans

2 cups boiling water

1 ounce dried porcini mushrooms

2 leeks, sliced

1 teaspoon canola oil

2 parsnips, diced

2 carrots, diced

2 stalks celery, diced

½ teaspoon ground fennel

1 teaspoon crushed rosemary

1 teaspoon dried chervil

⅛ teaspoon cloves

¼ teaspoon salt

¼ teaspoon freshly ground black pepper

2 cups Roasted Vegetable Stock (page 19)

1. The night before making the soup, place the beans in a 4-quart slow cooker. Fill with water to 1" below the top of the insert. Soak overnight.

2. Drain the beans and return them to the slow cooker. Pour the boiling water over the dried mushrooms in a heat-proof bowl and soak for 15 minutes. Slice only the white and light green parts of the leek into ¼" rounds. Cut the rounds in half.

3. Heat the oil in a nonstick skillet. Add the parsnip, carrots, celery, and leeks. Sauté for 1 minute, just until the color of the vegetables brightens. Add to the slow cooker along with the spices. Add the mushrooms, their soaking liquid, and the stock. Stir.

4. Cook on low for 8–10 hours.

PER SERVING Calories: 220 | Fat: 1.5g | Sodium: 170mg | Carbohydrates: 39g | Fiber: 10g | Protein: 15g

Stuffed Peppers

Try a mixture of green, red, orange, and yellow peppers for this dish.

INGREDIENTS | SERVES 4

4 large bell peppers

½ teaspoon ground chipotle pepper

¼ teaspoon hot Mexican chili powder

¼ teaspoon freshly ground black pepper

⅛ teaspoon salt

15 ounces canned fire-roasted diced tomatoes with garlic

1 cup cooked long-grain rice

1½ cups broccoli florets

¼ cup diced onion

½ cup water

1. Cut the tops off of each pepper to form a cap. Remove the seeds from the cap. Remove the seeds and most of the ribs inside the pepper. Place the peppers open-side up in an oval 4- or 6-quart slow cooker.

2. In a medium bowl, mix the spices, tomatoes, rice, broccoli, and onions. Spoon the mixture into each pepper until they are filled to the top. Replace the cap. Pour the water into the bottom of the slow cooker insert.

3. Cook on low for 6 hours.

PER SERVING Calories: 140 | Fat: 0.5g | Sodium: 580mg | Carbohydrates: 30g | Fiber: 5g | Protein: 4g

Palak Tofu

Palak tofu is a fresh-tasting, protein-rich Indian dish that is only slightly spicy.

INGREDIENTS | SERVES 4

14 ounces extra-firm tofu
1 tablespoon canola oil
1 teaspoon cumin seeds
2 cloves garlic, minced
2 jalapeños, minced
¾ pound red skin potatoes, diced
½ teaspoon ground ginger
¾ teaspoon garam masala
1 pound frozen cut-leaf spinach
¼ cup fresh cilantro

1. Cut the tofu into ½" cubes. Set aside.

2. Heat the oil in a nonstick skillet. Sauté the cumin seeds for 1 minute, then add the garlic and jalapeños. Sauté until fragrant, then add the tofu and potatoes. Sauté for 3 minutes. Add the ginger, garam masala, frozen spinach, and cilantro. Sauté 1 minute.

3. Pour the mixture into a 4-quart slow cooker and cook for 4 hours on low.

PER SERVING Calories: 190 | Fat: 7g | Sodium: 150mg | Carbohydrates: 22g | Fiber: 5g | Protein: 14g

Korean-Style Hot Pot

Serve this hot and spicy main dish with sides of steamed rice and kimchi.

INGREDIENTS | SERVES 8

3 bunches baby bok choy
8 cups water
8 ounces sliced crimini mushrooms
12 ounces extra-firm tofu, cubed
3 cloves garlic, thinly sliced
¼ teaspoon sesame oil
1 tablespoon crushed red pepper flakes
7 ounces enoki mushrooms

1. Remove the leaves of the baby bok choy. Wash thoroughly. Place them whole in a 4-quart slow cooker. Add the water, crimini mushrooms, tofu, garlic, sesame oil, and crushed red pepper. Stir.

2. Cook on low for 8 hours. Add the enoki mushrooms and stir. Cook an additional ½ hour before serving.

PER SERVING Calories: 80 | Fat: 2g | Sodium: 230mg | Carbohydrates: 11g | Fiber: 4g | Protein: 9g

Stuffed Eggplant

This easy vegan dish is a complete meal in itself.

INGREDIENTS | **SERVES 2**

1 1-pound eggplant
½ teaspoon olive oil
2 tablespoons minced red onion
1 clove garlic, minced
⅓ cup cooked rice
1 tablespoon fresh parsley
¼ cup corn kernels
¼ cup diced crimini mushrooms
15 ounces canned diced tomatoes with onions and garlic

1. Preheat oven to 375°F. Slice the eggplant in 2 equal halves, lengthwise. Use an ice cream scoop to take out the seeds. Place on a baking sheet, skin-side down. Bake for 8 minutes. Allow to cool slightly.

2. Heat the oil in a small skillet. Sauté the onions and garlic until softened.

3. In a medium bowl, stir the onions, garlic, rice, parsley, corn, and mushrooms. Divide evenly among the wells in the eggplant.

4. Pour the tomatoes onto the bottom of an oval 4- or 6-quart slow cooker. Place the eggplant halves side by side. Cook on low for 3 hours.

5. Remove the eggplants and plate. Drizzle with tomato sauce.

PER SERVING Calories: 190 | Fat: 3.5g | Sodium: 1,040mg | Carbohydrates: 41g | Fiber: 10g | Protein: 8g

Green Chile and Hominy Stew

Three green chiles make up with spicy yet comforting stew.

INGREDIENTS | SERVES 6

1 teaspoon canola oil
2 cubanelle peppers, diced
4 ounces canned diced green peppers
2 jalapeños, diced
1 onion, diced
4 cloves garlic, minced
3¾ cups water
24 ounces canned hominy
¼ teaspoon salt
½ teaspoon freshly ground black pepper
½ teaspoon ground jalapeño
3 zucchini, diced

1. Heat the oil in a nonstick pan. Sauté the cubanelle peppers, canned green peppers, jalapeños, onions, and garlic until fragrant.

2. Add the mixture to a 4-quart slow cooker. Add the water, hominy, salt, pepper, and ground jalapeño. Stir. Cook on low for 7 hours.

3. Add the zucchini and cook on high for 1 hour. Stir prior to serving.

PER SERVING Calories: 130 | Fat: 2g | Sodium: 420mg | Carbohydrates: 25g | Fiber: 5g | Protein: 4g

Hoppin' John

Hoppin' John is traditionally eaten on New Year's Day. Eating it as the first meal of the day is supposed to ensure health and prosperity for the coming year.

INGREDIENTS | SERVES 8

1 cup dried black-eyed peas, rehydrated

¾ cup water or Roasted Vegetable Stock (page 19)

1 teaspoon liquid smoke

1 teaspoon red pepper flakes

3 cups diced mustard or collard greens

14 ounces canned tomatoes

½ teaspoon freshly ground black pepper

¼ teaspoon salt

1 teaspoon dried oregano

Place all ingredients into a 4-quart slow cooker. Stir. Cook on high for 5 hours.

PER SERVING Calories: 70 | Fat: 0.5g | Sodium: 220mg | Carbohydrates: 12g | Fiber: 6g | Protein: 4g

Quick Prep for Black-Eyed Peas

Place in a large stockpot. Cover completely with water, and bring to a boil. Boil 2 minutes, reduce heat, and simmer for 1 hour.

Miso Soup with Tofu and Wakame

Traditionally, miso is never heated to boiling while making soup, making it a perfect dish to make in the slow cooker. Adding tofu and wakame seaweed makes it a complete meal.

INGREDIENTS | SERVES 6

2 quarts water

3–4 tablespoons white miso paste

12 ounces extra-firm tofu, diced

1 cup broken, dried wakame seaweed

1 bunch green onions, diced

1. Pour the water into a 4-quart slow cooker. Whisk in the miso paste until it is fully dissolved. Add the tofu. Cook on low for up to 8 hours.

2. Add the seaweed and green onion. Cook for 15 minutes on high. Stir before serving.

PER SERVING Calories: 60 | Fat: 1g | Sodium: 460mg | Carbohydrates: 6g | Fiber: 2g | Protein: 7g

CHAPTER 13

Side Dishes

Classic Baked Beans

This recipe is the perfect side dish for pulled pork or barbecue.

INGREDIENTS | **SERVES 12**

16 ounces dried navy beans

2 strips lean center-cut bacon or 2 strips turkey bacon

1 large onion, minced

4 cloves garlic, minced

2 tablespoons spicy mustard

2 teaspoons ground black pepper

1 teaspoon salt

3 tablespoons molasses

2 tablespoons dark brown sugar

1¼ cups water

½ cup chili sauce

½ teaspoon cloves

1. The night before you want to make the baked beans, place the dried beans in a 4-quart slow cooker and cover them with water. There should be at least 4" of water above the level of the beans. Soak overnight.

2. The next morning, fry the bacon until crisp, and then drain the slices on paper towel–lined plates. Crumble the bacon.

3. Drain the beans and return them to the slow cooker. Add the remaining ingredients. Stir to distribute all ingredients. Cook on low for 8–10 hours. Stir before serving.

PER SERVING Calories: 180 | Fat: 1g | Sodium: 580mg | Carbohydrates: 34g | Fiber: 10g | Protein: 9g

Stewed Squash

Crisp and fresh, this is the perfect summer side dish to show off the season's bounty.

INGREDIENTS | SERVES 4

1 medium onion, cut into ¼" slices
3 cups sliced zucchini
1 tablespoon fresh dill
3 tablespoons lemon juice
¼ teaspoon salt
¼ teaspoon black pepper
¾ cup fresh corn kernels
1 teaspoon butter

1. Place the onions on the bottom of a 1½- to 2-quart slow cooker. Top with zucchini, dill, lemon juice, salt, and pepper. Cook on low for 3½ hours.

2. Add the corn and butter and stir. Cook for an additional 30 minutes on high.

PER SERVING Calories: 70 | Fat: 1.5g | Sodium: 160mg | Carbohydrates: 14g | Fiber: 2g | Protein: 2g

Rosemary-Garlic Mashed Potatoes

Slow-cooked mashed potatoes are the perfect side for busy holiday cooks. Not only does this dish leave a burner free for other cooking, there is no need to boil the potatoes before mashing them.

INGREDIENTS | SERVES 10

3 pounds red skin potatoes, quartered
4 cloves garlic, minced
¾ cup Chicken Stock (page 17)
1 tablespoon minced, fresh rosemary
¼ cup 1% milk
1 tablespoon butter
⅓ cup reduced-fat sour cream

1. Place the potatoes in a 4-quart slow cooker. Add garlic, stock, and rosemary. Stir. Cover and cook on high until potatoes are tender, about 3–4 hours.

2. Pour in milk, butter, and sour cream. Mash with a potato masher.

PER SERVING Calories: 130 | Fat: 2.5g | Sodium: 50mg | Carbohydrates: 23g | Fiber: 2g | Protein: 4g

Red Beans and Rice

You could also serve this as a hearty vegetarian main dish.

INGREDIENTS | SERVES 8

1 teaspoon canola oil

1 small onion, diced

3 cloves garlic, minced

1 stalk celery, diced

15 ounces canned kidney beans, drained and rinsed

15 ounces canned diced tomatoes

4 ounces canned green chile

½ teaspoon dried oregano

½ teaspoon hot paprika

½ teaspoon cayenne pepper

½ teaspoon dried thyme

2 cups cooked long-grain rice

1. Heat the canola oil in a nonstick pan. Sauté the onions, garlic, and celery until the onions are soft, about 5 minutes.

2. Add the onion mixture, beans, tomatoes, chiles, and spices to a 1½- to 2-quart slow cooker. Cook on low for 6–8 hours. Remove the contents to a large bowl and stir in the rice.

PER SERVING Calories: 120 | Fat: 1g | Sodium: 240mg | Carbohydrates: 23g | Fiber: 4g | Protein: 5g

Tropical Baked Beans

No one will guess the secret ingredient in these baked beans!

INGREDIENTS | SERVES 12

1 pound dried navy beans
¼ cup cubed mango
1 large onion, diced
4 cloves garlic
½ cup chili sauce
½ cup water
1 tablespoon minced fresh ginger
1 tablespoon grainy mustard
1 teaspoon allspice
½ teaspoon cloves
½ teaspoon ground chipotle
½ teaspoon dried thyme
½ teaspoon freshly ground black pepper

1. The night before you want to make the baked beans, place the dried beans into a 4-quart slow cooker and cover with water. There should be at least 4" of water above the level of the beans. Soak overnight.

2. Drain the beans and return them to the slow cooker. Add the remaining ingredients. Stir to distribute all ingredients. Cook on low for 8–10 hours. Stir before serving.

PER SERVING Calories: 150 | Fat: 0.5g | Sodium: 330mg | Carbohydrates: 29g | Fiber: 10g | Protein: 9g

Loaded Mashed Potatoes

This recipe is a healthier version of the popular restaurant side dish.

INGREDIENTS | **SERVES 10**

3 pounds small russet potatoes, peeled

4 cloves garlic, sliced

1 medium onion, diced

1 tablespoon bacon bits

¾ cup water

¼ cup skim milk

¼ cup diced green onions

2 tablespoons grated Parmesan

¼ cup fat-free sour cream

1. Place the potatoes, garlic, onion, and bacon bits in a 4-quart slow cooker. Add water. Stir. Cover and cook on high until potatoes are tender, about 3–4 hours.

2. Add the milk, green onions, Parmesan, and sour cream. Mash with a potato masher.

PER SERVING Calories: 130 | Fat: 0.5g | Sodium: 45mg | Carbohydrates: 29g | Fiber: 2g | Protein: 5g

Using Dairy in the Slow Cooker

While evaporated milk is fine for long cooking times, cream, milk, and sour cream will curdle. Add them during the last part of the cooking time. Despite some advice, sweetened condensed milk cannot be used interchangeably with evaporated milk, cream, milk, or sour cream. It is very sweet and should never be used in savory dishes.

Wild Rice with Mixed Vegetables

Wild rice cooks up perfectly in the slow cooker. Try it as a high-fiber alternative to white rice or potatoes.

INGREDIENTS	SERVES 8

2½ cups water

1 cup wild rice

3 cloves garlic, minced

1 medium onion, diced

1 carrot, diced

1 stalk celery, diced

Place all ingredients into a 4-quart slow cooker and stir. Cover and cook on low for 4 hours. After 4 hours, check to see if the kernels are open and tender. If not, put the lid back on, and continue to cook for an additional 15–30 minutes. Stir before serving.

PER SERVING Calories: 90 | Fat: 0g | Sodium: 15mg | Carbohydrates: 18g | Fiber: 2g | Protein: 3g

Wild, Wild Rice

Wild rice is a bit of misnomer. It is actually a grass that grows in shallow water in North America. While it is often sold in mixes with white rice, it is also tasty all by itself.

Slimmed-Down Macaroni and Cheese

Although it is still a treat, this version of macaroni and cheese won't leave you feeling guilty. This method yields a very creamy dish that is easy to keep warm until everyone is ready for dinner.

INGREDIENTS	SERVES 6

1 teaspoon dry mustard

2 tablespoons cornstarch

¼ teaspoon freshly ground black pepper

2½ cups fat-free evaporated milk

1½ cups reduced-fat sharp Cheddar

8 ounces cooked macaroni

1. Spray a 4-quart slow cooker with nonstick cooking spray. In a small saucepan, heat the mustard, cornstarch, pepper, and evaporated milk until warmed through, whisking occasionally. Stir in the cheese.

2. Pour the macaroni into the slow cooker. Top with the cheese mixture and stir. Cover and cook on low for 1–2 hours or on high for 30 minutes.

PER SERVING Calories: 230 | Fat: 7g | Sodium: 125mg | Carbohydrates: 26g | Fiber: <1g | Protein: 17g

Salt-Baked Potatoes

Despite an abundance of salt, these potatoes are not salty at all, just perfectly cooked and tender.

INGREDIENTS | **SERVES 4**

Kosher salt, as needed
4 medium-to-large russet potatoes

Picking Potatoes

Different potatoes are good in different recipes. Red skin potatoes are soft and creamy, perfect for potato salads or mashing with the skin left on. Russet potatoes are starchier and are well suited to baking or making French fries.

1. Pour about ½" of salt into the bottom of an oval 4-quart slow cooker. Place the potatoes in a single layer on top of the salt. Add more salt until the potatoes are completely covered. Cover and cook on high for 2 hours or until the potatoes are fork-tender.

2. Crack the salt crust and remove the potatoes. Rub them with a towel to remove all of the salt before serving.

PER SERVING Calories: 290 | Fat: 0g | Sodium: 25mg | Carbohydrates: 64g | Fiber: 7g | Protein: 8g

Cuban Black Beans

*Traditionally served with rice, Cuban-style black beans are
also great served alongside Ropa Vieja (page 123).*

INGREDIENTS | **SERVES 4**

½ teaspoon apple cider vinegar
¼ cup diced onion
15 ounces canned black beans, drained and rinsed
2 cloves garlic, minced
1 jalapeño, minced
½ teaspoon oregano
¼ teaspoon cumin

1. Place all ingredients into a 2-quart slow cooker. Stir to distribute all the ingredients evenly.

2. Cook on low for 6–8 hours. Stir before serving.

PER SERVING Calories: 70 | Fat: 1g | Sodium: 530mg | Carbohydrates: 19g | Fiber: 6g | Protein: 4g

Dill Carrots

The carrots in this side dish keep a firm texture even when fully cooked.

INGREDIENTS | **SERVES 6**

1 pound carrots, cut into coin-sized pieces
1 tablespoon minced fresh dill
½ teaspoon butter
3 tablespoons water

1. Place all ingredients in a 2-quart slow cooker. Stir. Cook on low 1½–2 hours or until the carrots are fork tender.

2. Stir before serving.

PER SERVING Calories: 35 | Fat: 0g | Sodium: 40mg | Carbohydrates: 8g | Fiber: 2g | Protein: 1g

Dill Details

Dill is a delicate plant that has many culinary uses. The seeds are used as a spice, and fresh and dried dill, called dill weed, are used as herbs. Dill is an essential ingredient in dill pickles and gravlax, a type of cured salmon.

Rosemary-Thyme Green Beans

In this recipe, the slow cooker acts like a steamer, resulting in tender, crisp green beans.

INGREDIENTS | **SERVES 4**

1 pound green beans
1 tablespoon minced rosemary
1 teaspoon minced thyme
2 tablespoons lemon juice
2 tablespoons water

1. Place all ingredients into a 2-quart slow cooker. Stir to distribute the spices evenly.

2. Cook on low for 1½ hours or until the green beans are tender. Stir before serving.

PER SERVING Calories: 40 | Fat: 0g | Sodium: 5mg | Carbohydrates: 9g | Fiber: 4g | Protein: 2g

Three Bean Salad

This picnic favorite can be served hot or cold with equally delicious results.

INGREDIENTS | SERVES 12

15 ounces canned dark red kidney beans, drained and rinsed

15 ounces canned chickpeas, drained and rinsed

1 pound green beans

½ cup thinly sliced red onion

½ cup thinly sliced fennel

½ cup water

¼ teaspoon salt

¼ teaspoon freshly ground black pepper

1 teaspoon minced basil

2 tablespoons lemon juice

2 tablespoons Dijon mustard

2 tablespoons red wine vinegar

2 tablespoons olive oil

1 clove garlic, minced

1 teaspoon nonpareil capers

1. Place the kidney beans, chickpeas, green beans, red onion, fennel, and water into a 4-quart slow cooker. Cook on high 2 hours or 4 hours on low. Drain.

2. In a small bowl, whisk the salt, pepper, basil, lemon juice, mustard, vinegar, oil, garlic, and capers. Pour over the beans. Toss to coat.

PER SERVING Calories: 110 | Fat: 3g | Sodium: 350mg | Carbohydrates: 18g | Fiber: 5g | Protein: 5g

Capers Unmasked

Capers are the pickled bud of the caper plant. Capers are sold either in brine or packed in salt. If they are packed in salt, rinse them before using. Capers come in several sizes but only two are common in the United States: the larger capote caper and the smaller, more widely used nonpareil.

Potatoes Paprikash

This Hungarian classic is the perfect spicy side dish to serve with a roast.

INGREDIENTS | **SERVES 8**

1½ teaspoons olive oil

1 medium onion, halved and sliced

1 shallot, minced

4 cloves garlic, minced

½ teaspoon salt

½ teaspoon caraway seeds

¼ teaspoon freshly ground black pepper

1 teaspoon cayenne

3 tablespoons paprika

2 pounds red skin potatoes, thinly sliced

2 cups Chicken Stock (page 17) or Roasted Vegetable Stock (page 19)

2 tablespoons tomato paste

½ cup reduced-fat sour cream

1. Heat the oil in a nonstick pan. Sauté the onion, shallot, and garlic 1–2 minutes or until they begin to soften. Add the salt, caraway seeds, pepper, cayenne, and paprika, and stir. Immediately remove from heat.

2. Add the onion mixture, potatoes, stock, and tomato paste to a 4-quart slow cooker. Stir to coat the potatoes evenly. Cook on high for 2½ hours or until the potatoes are tender.

3. Turn off the heat and stir in the sour cream.

PER SERVING Calories: 160 | Fat: 4g | Sodium: 280mg | Carbohydrates: 27g | Fiber: 4g | Protein: 5g

Stewed Tomatoes

For an Italian variation, add basil and Italian parsley.

INGREDIENTS | SERVES 6

28 ounces whole tomatoes in purée, cut up
1 tablespoon minced onion
1 stalk celery, diced
½ teaspoon oregano
½ teaspoon thyme

Place all ingredients into a 2-quart slow cooker. Stir. Cook on low up to 8 hours.

PER SERVING Calories: 25 | Fat: 0g | Sodium: 180mg | Carbohydrates: 6g | Fiber: 1g | Protein: 1g

Sweet and Sour Red Cabbage

Even those who don't like cabbage will enjoy this dish; the cabbage's texture becomes meltingly soft.

INGREDIENTS | SERVES 6

½ head red cabbage, shredded
1 medium onion, shredded
1½ tablespoons dark brown sugar
1 teaspoon butter
¼ cup water
½ cup apple cider vinegar
1 tablespoon white wine vinegar
½ teaspoon freshly ground black pepper
¼ teaspoon salt
⅛ teaspoon ground cloves
½ teaspoon thyme

1. Place all ingredients into a 4-quart slow cooker. Stir to distribute all ingredients evenly.

2. Cook on low for 4–6 hours or until the cabbage is very soft. Stir before serving.

PER SERVING Calories: 60 | Fat: 1g | Sodium: 135mg | Carbohydrates: 13g | Fiber: 3g | Protein: 2g

Stewed Cinnamon Apples

These apples are wonderful with pork. The longer they are cooked, the softer they become.

INGREDIENTS | **SERVES 4**

1 teaspoon dark brown sugar

1 tablespoon ground cinnamon

2 tablespoons lemon juice

2 tablespoons water

4 crisp apples, cut into wedges

1. Place the sugar, cinnamon, lemon juice, and water into a 4-quart slow cooker. Stir until the sugar dissolves. Add the apples.

2. Cook on low for up to 8 hours. Stir before serving.

PER SERVING Calories: 90 | Fat: 0g | Sodium: 0mg | Carbohydrates: 25g | Fiber: 6g | Protein: 0g

Miso Eggplant

Miso Eggplant can be served hot or cold.

INGREDIENTS | **SERVES 4**

2 tablespoons water

¼ cup miso paste

1 1-pound eggplant, cubed

Place the water and miso into a 4-quart slow cooker. Stir to dissolve the miso. Add the eggplant and toss. Cook on high for 3 hours.

PER SERVING Calories: 60 | Fat: 0g | Sodium: 540mg | Carbohydrates: 12g | Fiber: 7g | Protein: 4g

Not-So-Mysterious Miso

Miso paste might seem exotic, but it is available in most grocery stores in the refrigerated section. Miso is produced by fermenting rice, barley, or soybeans, and is then made into a savory paste. It is most commonly used in soup but can be used to braise vegetables or on grilled dishes.

Stewed Okra

A Creole dish, this mixture of okra and tomatoes makes the most of seasonal ingredients.

INGREDIENTS | SERVES 4

2 large tomatoes, diced

1½ cups diced okra

1 small onion, diced

2 cloves garlic, minced

1 teaspoon hot sauce

Place all ingredients into a 2-quart slow cooker and stir. Cook on low for 2–3 hours. Stir before serving.

PER SERVING Calories: 40 | Fat: 0g | Sodium: 40mg | Carbohydrates: 8g | Fiber: 3g | Protein: 2g

Serving Okra

Okra has a distinctive pentagonal shape and a thick stem that should be discarded. When cooked, it releases a slippery, gooey substance. This can be off-putting to some but is easily counteracted by pairing the okra with something acidic, like tomatoes.

Mixed Summer Vegetables

The vegetables in this dish end up with a texture that is very close to steamed.

INGREDIENTS | SERVES 4

1 medium onion, cut into ¼" slices

1½ cups sliced zucchini

1½ cups sliced yellow squash

1 tablespoon minced fresh thyme

¼ cup lemon juice

¼ teaspoon salt

¼ teaspoon black pepper

¾ cup fresh corn kernels

½ cup diced okra

1 teaspoon butter

1. Place the onions on the bottom of a 1½- to 2-quart slow cooker. Top with zucchini, yellow squash, thyme, lemon juice, salt, and pepper. Cook on low for 3½ hours.

2. Add the corn, okra, and butter, and stir. Cook for an additional 30 minutes on high.

PER SERVING Calories: 80 | Fat: 1.5g | Sodium: 160mg | Carbohydrates: 16g | Fiber: 3g | Protein: 3g

Crimini Mushroom Un-Stuffing

"Stuffing" made in the slow cooker is moist and flavorful, the
next best thing to being roasted with the bird.

INGREDIENTS | **SERVES 18**

1½ tablespoons butter
1 pound onions, diced
1 pound celery, diced
8 ounces crimini mushrooms, sliced
12 cups cubed bread
1 egg
1 quart Chicken Stock (page 17)
½ tablespoon poultry seasoning
1 teaspoon marjoram
1 teaspoon dried sage
1 teaspoon dried parsley
1 teaspoon celery flakes
¼ teaspoon celery seeds
¼ teaspoon freshly ground black pepper
¼ teaspoon salt

1. Melt the butter in a large skillet. Sauté the onions, celery, and mushrooms until the onions are soft. Pour into a large bowl. Add the remaining ingredients and stir to combine.

2. Scoop into a 6-quart slow cooker, and cook on low for 6 hours.

PER SERVING Calories: 110 | Fat: 2.5g | Sodium: 300mg | Carbohydrates: 18g | Fiber: 2g | Protein: 4g

Gingered Sweet Potatoes

For this festive recipe, look for candied ginger that is not coated in sugar; it's called uncrystallized ginger.

INGREDIENTS | **SERVES 10**

2½ pounds sweet potatoes

1 cup water

1 tablespoon grated fresh ginger

½ tablespoon minced uncrystallized candied ginger

½ tablespoon butter

Sweet Potatoes or Yams?

Yams are not grown domestically, so the yams commonly found in supermarkets are actually varieties of sweet potato. True yams can be found in Asian or specialty stores and come in colors ranging from purple to yellow to white.

1. Peel and quarter the sweet potatoes. Add them to a 4-quart slow cooker. Add the water, fresh ginger, and candied ginger. Stir.

2. Cook on high for 3–4 hours or until the potatoes are tender. Add the butter and mash. Serve immediately or turn them down to low to keep warm for up to 3 hours.

PER SERVING Calories: 100 | Fat: 0.5g | Sodium: 65mg | Carbohydrates: 23g | Fiber: 3g | Protein: 2g

CHAPTER 14

Breakfast and Brunch

Southwestern Casserole

Serve this delicious dish with a poached egg on top.

INGREDIENTS | SERVES 6

4 large red potatoes, diced

1½ cups cubed 98% fat-free hickory-smoked ham

1 large onion, diced

1 jalapeño, seeded and diced

1 tablespoon butter

15 ounces canned diced tomatoes

4 ounces sliced button mushrooms

¼ teaspoon salt

¼ teaspoon pepper

¼ cup shredded reduced-fat Cheddar or Mexican-blend cheese mix

In a 4-quart slow cooker, stir all ingredients together, except the cheese. Cook on low for 8–9 hours. Stir in the cheese shortly before serving.

PER SERVING Calories: 280 | Fat: 5g | Sodium: 550mg | Carbohydrates: 46g | Fiber: 5g | Protein: 15g

Southern-Style Grits

Serve with eggs and bacon for a classic Southern breakfast. Refrigerate leftovers in meal-size portions and reheat them throughout the week.

INGREDIENTS | SERVES 12

1½ cups stone-ground grits

4¼ cups Chicken Stock (page 17) or water

½ teaspoon ground black pepper

¼ teaspoon salt

¼ cup shredded reduced-fat sharp Cheddar

Add the grits, stock, pepper, and salt to a 4-quart slow cooker. Stir. Cook on low for 8 hours. Stir the cheese into the grits before serving.

PER SERVING Calories: 80 | Fat: 0.5g | Sodium: 50mg | Carbohydrates: 16g | Fiber: 0g | Protein: 2g

Spinach and Canadian Bacon Breakfast Casserole

This casserole is more of a soufflé; the eggs puff up and the whole dish is delightfully light and fluffy. No one would guess how easy it is to make!

INGREDIENTS | SERVES 6

1 cup defrosted frozen spinach

1 teaspoon paprika

6 eggs

1½ cups fat-free evaporated milk

¼ cup diced green onion

1 cup shredded low-fat sharp Cheddar

4 ounces sliced Canadian bacon, diced

3 slices sandwich bread, cubed

1 cup sliced button or crimini mushrooms

Canadian Bacon versus American Bacon

American bacon is made from smoked and cured pork belly. It is high in fat and is known in other countries as "streaky bacon." Canadian bacon, as used in the United States, refers to bacon made from the pork loin. It is much lower in fat than American-style bacon.

1. Thoroughly squeeze out all water from the spinach. Spray a round 4-quart slow cooker with nonstick cooking spray. In a small bowl, whisk the paprika, eggs, evaporated milk, and green onion.

2. Sprinkle the bottom of the slow cooker with half of the cheese. Top with an even layer of spinach. Top that with a layer of half of the Canadian bacon. Add all of the bread cubes in one layer. Top with a layer of mushrooms, and then the remaining Canadian bacon. Sprinkle with the remaining cheese. Pour the egg mixture over the top and cover. Cook for 2 hours on high.

PER SERVING Calories: 230 | Fat: 8g | Sodium: 630mg | Carbohydrates: 17g | Fiber: 1g | Protein: 22g

Wheat Berry Breakfast

Serve this as-is or with a sprinkling of brown sugar on top.

INGREDIENTS | **SERVES 6**

1 cup wheat berries

2½ cups water

¼ cup sweetened, dried cranberries

What Are Wheat Berries?

Wheat berries are the entire kernel of wheat. Often ground into flour to be used in baking, wheat berries can also be eaten whole. They have a nutty flavor and a slightly chewy texture.

1. Add the wheat berries, water, and cranberries to a 2- or 4-quart slow cooker. Stir. Cook for 8–10 hours.

2. Stir before serving to distribute the cranberries evenly.

PER SERVING Calories: 120 | Fat: 3.5g | Sodium: 0mg | Carbohydrates: 27g | Fiber: 4g | Protein: 3g

Hearty Multigrain Cereal

Wake up to this high-fiber, satisfying breakfast!

INGREDIENTS | **SERVES 6**

¼ cup wheat berries

¼ cup long-grain rice

1 cup rolled or Irish-style oats

3½ cups water

Sweet or Savory Breakfast

Oatmeal and other hot breakfast cereals can be served two ways. The most popular is sweetened with a bit of sugar or fruit. An equally tasty way to eat your morning grains is to serve them savory; top the cereal with a small pat of butter and a small sprinkle of salt.

1. Add the wheat berries, rice, oats, and water to a 2- or 4-quart slow cooker. Stir. Cook for 8–10 hours.

2. Stir before serving.

PER SERVING Calories: 150 | Fat: 2.5g | Sodium: 0mg | Carbohydrates: 30g | Fiber: 4g | Protein: 5g

Spinach Quiche

This is an easy but festive dish that would be a perfect addition to brunch.

INGREDIENTS | SERVES 6

1 teaspoon ground cayenne pepper
4 eggs
½ cup shredded low-fat sharp Cheddar
6 ounces baby spinach
1½ cups fat-free evaporated milk
¼ cup diced green onion
2 slices sandwich bread, cubed

1. Spray a round 4-quart slow cooker with nonstick cooking spray. In a small bowl, whisk the cayenne, eggs, cheese, spinach, evaporated milk, and green onions.

2. Add the bread cubes in one layer on the bottom of the slow cooker. Pour the egg mixture over the top and cover. Cook for 2–3 hours on high or until the edges begin to pull away from the edge of the insert. Slice and lift out each slice individually.

PER SERVING Calories: 160 | Fat: 6g | Sodium: 220mg | Carbohydrates: 16g | Fiber: 2g | Protein: 13g

Breakfast Burrito Filling

Serve in a large tortilla with your favorite breakfast burrito toppings.

INGREDIENTS | SERVES 4

1¼ pounds lean boneless pork, cubed
12 ounces diced tomatoes with green chiles
1 small onion, diced
1 jalapeño, diced
½ teaspoon ground chipotle
¼ teaspoon cayenne pepper
¼ teaspoon ground jalapeño
2 cloves garlic, minced

Place all ingredients into a 2-quart slow cooker. Stir. Cook on low for 8 hours. Stir before serving.

PER SERVING Calories: 310 | Fat: 12g | Sodium: 430mg | Carbohydrates: 6g | Fiber: 1g | Protein: 44g

Hash Browns

*Also called home fries, this home-style dish will serve four
as a main dish, or six if part of a hardy breakfast.*

INGREDIENTS | **SERVES 4**

1 teaspoon canola oil

2 strips turkey bacon, diced

1 large onion, thinly sliced

1½ pounds red skin potatoes, thinly sliced

1. Heat oil in a nonstick skillet. Add bacon, onions, and potatoes. Sauté until just browned. The potatoes should not be fully cooked.

2. Add mixture to a 2- or 4-quart slow cooker. Cook on low for 3–4 hours or on high for 1½ hours.

PER SERVING Calories: 170 | Fat: 3g | Sodium: 95mg | Carbohydrates: 31g | Fiber: 3g | Protein: 5g

Pear Oatmeal

*Cooking rolled oats overnight makes them so creamy they could be served
as dessert. Cooking them with fruit is just the icing on the cake.*

INGREDIENTS | **SERVES 4**

2 Bosc pears, cored and thinly sliced

2¼ cups pear cider or water

1½ cups old-fashioned rolled oats

1 tablespoon dark brown sugar

½ teaspoon cinnamon

Place all ingredients in a 4-quart slow cooker. Cook on low overnight (8–9 hours). Stir and serve.

PER SERVING Calories: 220 | Fat: 2.5g | Sodium: 0mg | Carbohydrates: 43g | Fiber: 7g | Protein: 6g

A Quick Guide to Oatmeal

Oat groats are oats that still have the bran, but the outer husk has been removed. Rolled oats are groats that have been rolled into flat flakes for quick cooking, a process that removes the bran. Scottish oats are oat groats that have been chopped to include the bran. Quick-cooking or instant oats are more processed rolled oats.

French Toast Casserole

This recipe is great for breakfast, and it's a wonderful way to use bread that is slightly stale.

INGREDIENTS | SERVES 8

12 slices whole-meal raisin bread
6 eggs
1 teaspoon vanilla
2 cups fat-free evaporated milk
2 tablespoons dark brown sugar
1 teaspoon cinnamon
¼ teaspoon nutmeg

1. Spray a 4-quart slow cooker with nonstick spray. Layer the bread in the slow cooker.

2. In a small bowl, whisk the eggs, vanilla, evaporated milk, brown sugar, cinnamon, and nutmeg. Pour over the bread.

3. Cover and cook on low for 6–8 hours. Remove the lid and cook uncovered for 30 minutes or until the liquid has evaporated.

PER SERVING Calories: 230 | Fat: 6g | Sodium: 280mg | Carbohydrates: 32g | Fiber: 2g | Protein: 13g

Breakfast Quinoa with Fruit

Take a break from oatmeal and try this fruity quinoa instead!

INGREDIENTS | SERVES 4

1 cup quinoa
2 cups water
½ cup dried mixed berries
1 pear, thinly sliced
1 teaspoon dark brown sugar
½ teaspoon ground ginger
¼ teaspoon cinnamon
⅛ teaspoon cloves
⅛ teaspoon nutmeg

Place all ingredients into a 4-quart slow cooker. Stir. Cook for 2–3 hours or until the quinoa is fully cooked.

PER SERVING Calories: 250 | Fat: 3g | Sodium: 10mg | Carbohydrates: 51g | Fiber: 5g | Protein: 6g

Pear, Apple, and Cranberry Pancake Topping

Add this festive topping to pancakes to make breakfast a real treat!

INGREDIENTS | SERVES 8

3 tart apples, thinly sliced

3 Bosc pears, thinly sliced

¾ cup fresh cranberries

1 tablespoon brown sugar

½ teaspoon ground ginger

½ teaspoon cinnamon

¼ teaspoon nutmeg

¼ teaspoon mace

Place all ingredients into a 2-quart slow cooker. Stir. Cook on low for 2 hours.

PER SERVING Calories: 70 | Fat: 0g | Sodium: 0mg | Carbohydrates: 19g | Fiber: 4g | Protein: 0g

Crantastic!

Cranberries are a superfood. High in antioxidants and fiber, they are a welcome addition to both sweet and savory dishes. They are also naturally high in pectin, which means they'll thicken any dish.

Cheese "Soufflé"

Try this slimmed-down, no-fuss version of soufflé at your next brunch.

INGREDIENTS | SERVES 8

8 ounces reduced-fat sharp Cheddar, shredded

8 ounces skim-milk mozzarella, shredded

8 slices thin sandwich bread

2 cups fat-free evaporated milk

4 eggs

¼ teaspoon cayenne

1. Mix the cheeses, and set aside. Tear the bread into large pieces, and set aside. Spray a 4-quart slow cooker with nonstick cooking spray. Alternately layer the cheese and bread in the insert, beginning and ending with bread.

2. In a small bowl, whisk the evaporated milk, eggs, and cayenne. Pour over the bread and cheese layers. Cook on low for 2–3 hours.

PER SERVING Calories: 310 | Fat: 16g | Sodium: 390mg | Carbohydrates: 20g | Fiber: 0g | Protein: 25g

Ham and Egg Casserole

Slow cooker breakfasts ensure a hot breakfast even on the busiest of mornings. This high-protein breakfast will see you through until lunch.

INGREDIENTS | **SERVES 6**

6 eggs
½ teaspoon freshly ground black pepper
¼ teaspoon paprika
⅓ cup shredded sharp Cheddar
4 ounces canned diced green chiles, drained
3 ounces 98% fat-free smoked ham slice, diced
2 slices thin sandwich bread

1. In a small bowl, whisk the eggs, spices, Cheddar, and chiles. Stir in the ham. Set aside.

2. Spray a 2-quart slow cooker with nonstick cooking spray. Place the bread in a single layer on the bottom of the insert. Pour the egg mixture on top.

3. Cook for 7 hours on low. Use a spatula to separate the egg from the sides of the slow cooker. Lift the whole casserole out of the insert. Place it on a cutting board and slice it into six equal slices.

PER SERVING Calories: 140 | Fat: 8g | Sodium: 410mg | Carbohydrates: 5g | Fiber: <1g | Protein: 11g

CHAPTER 15

For a Crowd

Slow-Roasted Chicken with Potatoes, Parsnips, and Onions

*Chicken made in the slow cooker is very tender. The onions
add a lot of flavor with no added fat needed.*

INGREDIENTS | SERVES 6

4 medium onions, sliced
1 6-pound roasting chicken
6 large red skin potatoes, halved
4 parsnips, diced
1 teaspoon salt
1 teaspoon black pepper

A Snippet about Parsnips

Parsnips have a mild flavor and a texture
that is well suited to extended cooking
times. Always peel off the bitter skin
before cooking. If parsnips are not available, carrots are an acceptable substitute.

1. Cover the bottom of a 6- to 7-quart oval slow cooker with half of the onions.

2. Place the chicken, breast-side up, on top of the onions.

3. Cover the chicken with the remaining onions.

4. Arrange the potatoes and parsnips around the chicken.

5. Cover and cook on low for 8 hours or until the chicken has an internal temperature of 165°F as measured using a food thermometer. Discard the chicken skin before serving.

PER SERVING Calories: 730 | Fat: 10g | Sodium: 540mg |
Carbohydrates: 86g | Fiber: 11g | Protein: 71g

Lasagna with Spinach

There is no need to precook the noodles in this recipe.

INGREDIENTS | **SERVES 10**

28 ounces fat-free ricotta cheese

1 cup defrosted frozen cut spinach

1 egg

½ cup part-skim shredded mozzarella cheese

8 cups Marinara Sauce (page 189)

½ pound uncooked regular lasagna noodles

1. In a medium bowl, stir the ricotta, spinach, egg, and mozzarella.

2. Ladle a quarter of the marinara sauce along the bottom of a 6-quart oval slow cooker. The bottom should be thoroughly covered in sauce. Add a single layer of lasagna noodles on top of the sauce, breaking noodles if needed to fit in the sides.

3. Ladle an additional quarter of sauce over the noodles, covering all of the noodles. Top with half of the cheese mixture, pressing firmly with the back of a spoon to smooth. Add a single layer of lasagna noodles on top of the cheese, breaking noodles if needed to fit in the sides.

4. Ladle another quarter of the sauce on top of the noodles, and top with the remaining cheese. Press another layer of noodles onto the cheese and top with the remaining sauce. Take care that the noodles are entirely covered in sauce.

5. Cover and cook for 4–6 hours until cooked through.

PER SERVING Calories: 180 | Fat: 2.5g | Sodium: 160mg | Carbohydrates: 26g | Fiber: 2g | Protein: 13g

Braciola

Look for steaks that are approximately ⅛" thick, 8"–10" long, and 5" wide to make this Italian roulade.

INGREDIENTS | **SERVES 8**

½ teaspoon olive oil

½ cup diced onions

2 cloves garlic, minced

32 ounces canned diced tomatoes

8 stalks rapini

8 very thin-cut round steaks (about 1¼ pounds total)

4 teaspoons bread crumbs

4 teaspoons grated Parmesan

1. Heat the oil in a nonstick pan. Sauté the onions and garlic until the onions are soft, about 5 minutes. Place in a 6-quart oval slow cooker. Add the tomatoes and stir to combine.

2. Cut the stems off the rapini. Place the steaks on a platter horizontally. Sprinkle each steak with ½ teaspoon bread crumbs and ½ teaspoon Parmesan. Place a bunch of rapini leaves on one end of each steak. Roll each steak toward the other end. It should look like a spiral. Place in the skillet seam-side down. Cook for 1 minute, use tongs to flip the steaks carefully, and cook the other side for 1 minute.

3. Place each roll in a single layer on top of the tomato sauce. Cook on low for 1–2 hours or until the steaks are cooked through.

PER SERVING Calories: 160 | Fat: 6g | Sodium: 115mg | Carbohydrates: 9g | Fiber: 2g | Protein: 18g

Blackberry Pulled Pork

The blackberry seeds are very soft after the long cooking time, but if you want a smoother sauce, press the blackberries through a mesh sieve before adding them to the slow cooker. Discard the seeds.

INGREDIENTS | **SERVES 12**

6 pounds boneless pork roast, excess fat removed

2 cups fresh blackberries

½ cup chili sauce

½ cup balsamic vinegar

¼ teaspoon lime juice

1 tablespoon ginger preserves

2 teaspoons mesquite liquid smoke

2 teaspoons freshly ground black pepper

1 teaspoon ground cayenne

1 teaspoon chili powder

1 teaspoon hot paprika

2 large onions, diced

5 cloves garlic, minced

¼ teaspoon salt

1. Place all ingredients in a 6-quart slow cooker. Cook on low for 8–9 hours or on high for 6 hours.

2. When done, the meat should shred easily with a fork. Remove the pork from the slow cooker. Shred with a fork and set aside. Mash any solid bits of the sauce in the slow cooker with a potato masher. Return the pork to the slow cooker, and toss to coat the pork evenly with the sauce.

PER SERVING Calories: 510 | Fat: 19g | Sodium: 510mg | Carbohydrates: 13g | Fiber: 2g | Protein: 68g

Goan Chicken Curry

This Indian dish is made easily in the slow cooker. Try it over rice or with some naan.

INGREDIENTS | SERVES 10

1 teaspoon canola oil

2 medium onions, diced

4 cloves garlic, minced

3 pounds boneless, skinless chicken thighs, cubed

1 tablespoon minced fresh ginger

2 cups toasted unsweetened coconut

1 teaspoon ground cinnamon

¼ teaspoon ground nutmeg

½ teaspoon ground cloves

½ teaspoon salt

1 teaspoon cumin seeds

1 teaspoon black mustard seeds

2 tablespoons red pepper flakes

1½ cups water

1. In a large nonstick skillet, heat the oil. Sauté the onions and garlic for 3 minutes.

2. Place all ingredients in a 6-quart slow cooker. Stir. Cover and cook for 6–8 hours on low. Stir before serving.

PER SERVING Calories: 480 | Fat: 33g | Sodium: 230mg | Carbohydrates: 11g | Fiber: 6g | Protein: 37g

How to Toast Coconut

Preheat the oven to 350°F. Arrange shredded coconut on a single layer on a cookie sheet. Bake for 10–15 minutes or until light golden brown. Stir the coconut and check it frequently to prevent burning. Remove it from the oven and allow it to cool before using.

Greek Boneless Leg of Lamb

Lamb does surprisingly well in the slow cooker. It is nearly impossible to overcook, and every bite is meltingly tender.

INGREDIENTS | SERVES 12

4 pounds boneless leg of lamb
1 tablespoon crushed rosemary
1 teaspoon freshly ground black pepper
¼ teaspoon kosher salt
¼ cup lemon juice
¼ cup water

1. Slice off any visible fat from the lamb and discard. Place in a 4- or 6-quart slow cooker.

2. Add the remaining ingredients on top of the lamb. Cook on low for 8 hours.

3. Remove from the slow cooker. Discard cooking liquid. Remove any remaining visible fat from the lamb. Slice the lamb prior to serving.

PER SERVING Calories: 350 | Fat: 21g | Sodium: 150mg | Carbohydrates: 1g | Fiber: 0g | Protein: 38g

Healthy Cooking with Lamb

Lamb has a reputation as a somewhat fatty meat. However, buying a leaner cut, like the boneless leg where much of the fat and bone has been removed by the butcher, and slicing off any excess at home can eliminate much of the fat. When slow cooking, the fat melts off the meat and accumulates in the bottom of the cooker where it can easily be discarded after removing the meat.

Hawaiian-Style Mahi-Mahi

The fish is gently poached in a flavorful liquid, which infuses it with flavor.

INGREDIENTS | SERVES 6

6 4-ounce mahi-mahi fillets
12 ounces pineapple juice
3 tablespoons grated fresh ginger
¼ cup lime juice
3 tablespoons ponzu sauce

1. Place the fillets in a 6-quart slow cooker. Top with the remaining ingredients. Cook on low 5 hours or until the fish is fully cooked.

2. Remove the fillets and discard the cooking liquid.

PER SERVING Calories: 140 | Fat: 1g | Sodium: 100mg | Carbohydrates: 10g | Fiber: 0g | Protein: 21g

Slow Cooking with Fish

Fish is fabulous in the slow cooker. The fish stays moist and cooks evenly as long as there at least some liquid in the insert.

Low Country Boil

Popular in Georgia and the Carolinas, Low Country Boil is the perfect one-pot meal for a summer day.

INGREDIENTS | SERVES 8

4 ears corn, halved
1½ pounds baby red skin potatoes
¼ cup Chesapeake Bay seasoning or shrimp boil seasoning
1 tablespoon yellow mustard seeds
2 large onions, thinly sliced
1 bay leaf
Water, as needed
1½ pounds medium shrimp

1. Place the corn, potatoes, seasoning, mustard seeds, onions, and bay leaf into a 6- or 7-quart slow cooker. Fill the insert with water until it is about 2½" below the top edge of the insert.

2. Cook for 2½ hours on high or until the corn and potatoes are tender. Add the shrimp and continue to cook on high for 20 minutes or until thoroughly cooked.

PER SERVING Calories: 240 | Fat: 3g | Sodium: 280mg | Carbohydrates: 30g | Fiber: 3g | Protein: 21g

Shredded Beef for Sandwiches

Due to the long cooking time, it is possible to prepare the meat late the night before serving so it will be ready to eat for lunch.

INGREDIENTS | SERVES 16

4¼ pounds lean boneless beef roast, excess fat removed

1 onion, chopped

3 cloves garlic, chopped

1 teaspoon paprika

1 teaspoon chili powder

½ teaspoon celery seed

½ teaspoon dried tarragon

½ teaspoon dried mustard

½ teaspoon freshly ground black pepper

¼ teaspoon salt

1 tablespoon hot sauce

1 tablespoon hickory liquid smoke

½ cup water

1. Place all ingredients into a 6- to 7-quart slow cooker. Cook on low for 10–12 hours. The meat should be easily shredded with a fork.

2. Remove the meat from the slow cooker to a plate. Shred with a fork. Mash the contents of the slow cooker with a potato masher. Return the beef to the slow cooker and stir to distribute the ingredients evenly.

PER SERVING Calories: 430 | Fat: 34g | Sodium: 140mg | Carbohydrates: 1g | Fiber: 0g | Protein: 28g

Ask the Butcher

If the beef sitting on the shelf of the local store is too fatty, ask the butcher to cut a fresh leaner cut. You won't have to do fat removal at home, which can be tricky depending on the cut of meat. The butcher can also suggest lean beef alternatives to fattier cuts.

Italian Meatloaf

Meatloaf made in the slow cooker is amazingly moist and tender. The onion layer on the bottom prevents the meatloaf from sitting directly in any fat that drains off.

INGREDIENTS | SERVES 10

1 large onion, cut into rings
2 pounds 94% lean ground beef
1 egg
¼ cup bread crumbs
1 tablespoon Italian herb mix
1 teaspoon dried oregano
1 teaspoon crushed red pepper flakes
1 teaspoon ground fennel seed
1 teaspoon crushed rosemary
¼ teaspoon freshly ground black pepper
⅛ teaspoon salt
½ cup diced onion
1 clove garlic, minced
¼ cup dry-packed sun-dried tomatoes, diced
3 ounces tomato paste
1 tablespoon Worcestershire sauce

1. Spray a 6-quart oval slow cooker with cooking spray. Line the bottom of the pan with the onion rings.

2. In a large bowl, mix the ground beef, egg, bread crumbs, Italian herb mix, oregano, red pepper flakes, fennel seed, rosemary, pepper, salt, diced onion, garlic, and sun-dried tomatoes until well combined. Mold into a loaf shape and place on top of the sliced onions.

3. In a small bowl, whisk the tomato paste and Worcestershire sauce. Brush over the top and visible sides of the meatloaf.

4. Cook for 4–6 hours on low or until the meat is thoroughly cooked. Remove the meatloaf from the slow cooker and slice. Discard the onion rings and any juices on the bottom of the pan.

PER SERVING Calories: 170 | Fat: 6g | Sodium: 250mg | Carbohydrates: 8g | Fiber: 1g | Protein: 21g

Southwestern Meatloaf Variation

Substitute ⅓ cup black beans for the sun-dried tomatoes. Also substitute 1 teaspoon each of ground chipotle pepper, hot paprika, and ground jalapeño for the oregano, Italian herb mix, rosemary, and fennel. For the topping, whisk the tomato paste with 1 teaspoon hot sauce and 1 teaspoon water.

Spiced Cider

The aroma of this warming cider will fill your whole house!

INGREDIENTS | **SERVES 20**

2 cinnamon sticks

1" chunk fresh ginger

1 tablespoon whole cloves

1 gallon apple cider

1 tablespoon dark brown sugar

½ teaspoon ground nutmeg

How to Make a Cheesecloth Packet

Place the items to be enclosed in the packet on a length of cheesecloth. Cut out a square about three times larger than the area the items take up. Pull all ends toward the middle and tie closed with kitchen twine.

1. Place the cinnamon sticks, ginger, and cloves into a cheesecloth packet. Place the packet, cider, brown sugar, and nutmeg into a 6-quart slow cooker. Stir until the sugar dissolves.

2. Cook on high for 2–3 hours or until very hot. Reduce to low to keep hot until or during serving. Remove packet after cooking if desired.

PER SERVING Calories: 100 | Fat: 0g | Sodium: 20mg | Carbohydrates: 25g | Fiber: 0g | Protein: 0g

Pot Roast with Root Vegetables

A variety of autumnal vegetables make this pot roast a complete meal in one.

INGREDIENTS | SERVES 12

1 cup water
4 russet potatoes, quartered
4 carrots, cut into thirds
4 parsnips, quartered
3 rutabagas, quartered
2 onions, sliced
1 celeriac, cubed
7 cloves garlic, sliced
4 pounds lean top round beef roast, excess fat removed
½ teaspoon salt
1 teaspoon paprika
½ teaspoon freshly ground black pepper

1. Pour the water into an oval 6-quart slow cooker. Add the potatoes, carrots, parsnips, rutabagas, onions, celeriac, and garlic. Stir.

2. Add the beef. Sprinkle with salt, paprika, and pepper. Cook on low for 8 hours.

3. Remove and slice the beef. Use a slotted spoon to serve the vegetables. Discard the cooking liquid.

PER SERVING Calories: 310 | Fat: 5g | Sodium: 230mg | Carbohydrates: 36g | Fiber: 7g | Protein: 36g

Pork Tenderloin with Fennel

Slightly sweet fennel accents the pork's natural sweetness.

INGREDIENTS | SERVES 10

4 pounds pork tenderloin, excess fat removed

4 bulbs fennel, cubed

1½ cups Caramelized Onions (page 16)

1 teaspoon freshly ground black pepper

½ teaspoon salt

Place the pork into an oval 6- to 7-quart slow cooker. Top with remaining ingredients. Cook on low for 8 hours.

PER SERVING Calories: 250 | Fat: 7g | Sodium: 260mg | Carbohydrates: 7g | Fiber: 3g | Protein: 39g

Tomato Sauce with Sausage

This classic sauce is perfect to take to a potluck; it can feed a crowd with minimal cost and effort.

INGREDIENTS | SERVES 15

2 teaspoons olive oil

2 onions, diced

2 carrots, diced

5 cloves garlic, diced

2 pounds Italian chicken or turkey sausages, sliced

56 ounces canned crushed tomatoes

30 ounces canned diced tomatoes

3 ounces tomato paste

2 tablespoons red pepper flakes

¼ cup minced fresh basil

¼ cup minced Italian parsley

1. Heat the oil in a nonstick pan. Sauté the onions, carrots, garlic, and sausage until the onion is translucent and soft. Drain off any excess fat.

2. Place the tomatoes and tomato paste into a 6- to 7-quart slow cooker. Stir in the red pepper flakes and basil. Add the sausage mixture. Cook on low for 8 hours. Stir in the parsley. Serve immediately.

PER SERVING Calories: 170 | Fat: 6g | Sodium: 570mg | Carbohydrates: 16g | Fiber: 4g | Protein: 14g

Sticky Spicy Spare Ribs

Broiling the ribs removes most of the fat, but they still get very tender in the slow cooker.

INGREDIENTS | SERVES 8

4 pounds lean pork spare ribs
2 tablespoons dark brown sugar
½ cup chili sauce
¼ cup rice vinegar
¼ cup garlic-chili sauce
1 shallot, minced

1. Place the ribs on a broiler-safe platter. Broil on high until much of the fat has been rendered. Place in a 6- to 7-quart slow cooker.

2. In a small bowl, whisk the brown sugar, chili sauce, rice vinegar, garlic-chili sauce, and shallot. Pour over the ribs. Cook for 8 hours.

3. Remove spare ribs from the slow cooker. Place them on a baking sheet in a cold oven to keep warm. Transfer sauce to a small bowl. Drain off fat. Pour over the ribs before serving.

PER SERVING Calories: 410 | Fat: 19g | Sodium: 870mg | Carbohydrates: 13 | Fiber: 0g | Protein: 44g

Thyme-Roasted Turkey Breast

Slow-cooked turkey is so moist there's no basting required!

INGREDIENTS | **SERVES 10**

2 onions, thinly sliced

1 6- to 7-pound turkey breast or turkey half

½ cup minced thyme

½ tablespoon freshly ground black pepper

½ tablespoon salt

½ tablespoon dried parsley

½ tablespoon celery flakes

½ tablespoon mustard seed

1. Arrange the onion slices in a thin layer on the bottom of a 6- to 7-quart slow cooker.

2. Make a small slit in the skin of the turkey and spread the thyme between the skin and meat. Smooth the skin back onto the turkey.

3. In a small bowl, stir the pepper, salt, parsley, celery flakes, and mustard seed. Rub the spice mixture into the skin of the turkey.

4. Place the turkey in the slow cooker on top of the onion layer. Cook for 8 hours. Remove the skin and onions and discard them before serving the turkey.

PER SERVING Calories: 450 | Fat: 19g | Sodium: 520mg | Carbohydrates: 4g | Fiber: 1g | Protein: 60g

Greek-Style Meatballs and Artichokes

Mediterranean flavors abound in this dish. Serve it with an orzo pilaf.

INGREDIENTS | SERVES 10

2 thin slices white sandwich bread

½ cup 1% milk

2¾ pounds lean ground pork

2 cloves garlic, minced

1 egg

½ teaspoon lemon zest

¼ teaspoon freshly ground pepper

16 ounces frozen artichoke hearts, defrosted

3 tablespoons lemon juice

2 cups Chicken Stock (page 17)

¾ cup frozen chopped spinach

⅓ cup sliced Greek olives

1 tablespoon minced fresh oregano

1. Preheat the oven to 350°F. Place the bread and milk in a shallow saucepan. Cook on low until the milk is absorbed, about 1 minute. Place into a large bowl and add the pork, garlic, egg, zest, and pepper.

2. Mix until all ingredients are evenly distributed. Roll into 1" balls. Line two baking sheets with parchment paper. Place the meatballs in a single layer on the baking sheets. Bake for 15 minutes, and then drain on paper towel–lined plates.

3. Add the meatballs to a 6- to 7-quart slow cooker. Add the remaining ingredients.

4. Cook on low for 6–8 hours.

PER SERVING Calories: 400 | Fat: 28g | Sodium: 340mg | Carbohydrates: 9g | Fiber: <1g | Protein: 25g

Steak Carnitas

Carnitas are delicious wrapped in tortillas. Serve with shredded iceberg lettuce, diced tomatoes, diced onion, and cilantro.

INGREDIENTS | SERVES 10

1½ pounds lean bottom round, cubed

3 cloves garlic, minced

1 jalapeño, minced

¼ cup habanero salsa

¼ teaspoon salt

¼ teaspoon freshly ground black pepper

2 teaspoons ground chipotle

1 teaspoon New Mexican chili powder

½ teaspoon oregano

2 tablespoons lime juice

2 tablespoons orange juice

1 tablespoon lime zest

1. Quickly brown the beef in a nonstick skillet. Add to a 4-quart slow cooker.

2. In a small bowl, whisk the rest of the ingredients. Pour over the beef. Stir.

3. Cook on low for 6 hours, remove the cover, and cook on high for 30 minutes. Stir before serving.

PER SERVING Calories: 140 | Fat: 8g | Sodium: 140mg | Carbohydrates: 3g | Fiber: <1g | Protein: 14g

Juice Citrus with Ease

Here are a few tips to get the most juice out of citrus. Microwave the whole fruit for 20 seconds before juicing. Roll the fruit on the countertop before you squeeze it. After squeezing the fruit the first time, use a knife to slice the membranes and squeeze it again to extract even more juice.

Jerk Chicken

Virtually no hands-on time makes this recipe a breeze.

INGREDIENTS | **SERVES 12**

3 pounds boneless, skinless chicken breast or thighs

3 tablespoons Jamaican jerk seasoning

1 Scotch bonnet pepper, sliced

¼ cup fresh thyme leaves

½ cup lemon juice

1 onion, chopped

1 clove garlic, minced

1 teaspoon hickory liquid smoke

½ teaspoon ground allspice

¼ teaspoon cloves

Place the chicken on the bottom of a 6- to 7-quart slow cooker. Pour the remaining ingredients on top. Cook on low for 5 hours.

PER SERVING Calories: 180 | Fat: 3.5g | Sodium: 280mg | Carbohydrates: 3g | Fiber: <1g | Protein: 33g

Easy Mornings

Cut up vegetables in the evening and refrigerate them overnight. If cutting and storing meat, place it in a separate container from the vegetables to avoid cross contamination. To save even more time, you can measure out dry spices and leave them in the slow cooker insert overnight.

Osso Bucco

Osso Bucco is an extremely inexpensive yet chic dish to make. The slow cooker takes a lot of the work out of making this classic dish.

INGREDIENTS | SERVES 12

1 cup flour

1 teaspoon freshly ground black pepper

6 pounds veal shanks (12 shanks)

1 tablespoon olive oil

1 tablespoon butter

2 cups chopped onion

8 cloves garlic, minced

2 anchovies

2 tablespoons minced fresh rosemary

2 tablespoons minced fresh thyme

6 cups beef broth

Soaking and the Slow Cooker

If there is food stuck inside your slow cooker's insert, don't be tempted to soak it in the sink overnight. If your slow cooker has an unglazed bottom, it will absorb water, which may lead to cracking. Instead, place the slow cooker on the counter and use a pitcher to fill it with water.

1. In a shallow bowl, mix together the flour and pepper. Dredge the veal shanks in flour. Set aside.

2. Heat the oil in a nonstick skillet. Brown the veal shanks on all sides. Drain off all the grease. Drain the veal on paper towel-–lined plates, and then place the shanks in a 6- to 7-quart slow cooker.

3. Heat the butter in a large pan. Sauté the onions, garlic, and anchovies for 3 minutes. Add the rosemary, thyme, and broth. Bring to a boil. Boil for 5–8 minutes or until the mixture starts to reduce. Pour over the veal shanks. Cook on low for 9 hours.

4. Skim off any fat that has risen to the top. Divide the shanks and drizzle each with ¼ cup broth. Discard remaining broth.

PER SERVING Calories: 330 | Fat: 9g | Sodium: 910mg | Carbohydrates: 13g | Fiber: <1g | Protein: 46g

Portobello Tri-Tip

Lean, often overlooked cuts of beef like the tri-tip are perfect for the slow cooker. The long, moisture-rich environment creates tender meat, despite the lack of fat.

INGREDIENTS | **SERVES 12**

3 pounds tri-tip, excess fat removed

6 Portobello mushroom caps, sliced

1 onion, diced

1 tablespoon Canadian Steak Seasoning

¼ cup beef broth

1 tablespoon Worcestershire sauce

1 tablespoon balsamic vinegar

Make Your Own Canadian Steak Seasoning

In a small bowl, stir 2 tablespoons each black pepper, kosher salt, caraway seeds, paprika, granulated garlic, and dehydrated mushrooms. Store in an airtight container. Mix into hamburgers or meatloaf or use as a dry rub on steaks.

1. In a dry skillet, sear each side of the tri-tip. Place in a 6- to 7-quart slow cooker.

2. Spray a nonstick pan with cooking spray. Sauté mushrooms and onions until the onions are soft but not browned. Add to the slow cooker, along with the remaining ingredients.

3. Cook on low for 6–8 hours or until the meat is falling apart and tender.

PER SERVING Calories: 220 | Fat: 12g | Sodium: 280mg | Carbohydrates: 4g | Fiber: <1g | Protein: 25g

Chicken and Sausage Paella

This simplified paella is an elegant addition to any dinner party; no specialty paella pan needed!

INGREDIENTS | **SERVES 8**

2 cups cubed cooked chicken breast

8 ounces fully cooked chicken andouille sausage, cut into 1" pieces

2½ quarts Chicken Stock (page 17)

1½ cups frozen peas

2 carrots, diced

12 ounces long-grain rice

1 onion, diced

1 teaspoon crushed saffron

1 teaspoon smoked paprika

1½ cups raw shrimp

1. Place the chicken breast, sausage, stock, peas, carrots, rice, onions, saffron, and paprika in a 6- to 7-quart slow cooker. Cook on high for 2 hours.

2. Add the shrimp and continue to cook on high for 30 minutes or until the shrimp is fully cooked. Stir prior to serving.

PER SERVING Calories: 440 | Fat: 10g | Sodium: 800mg | Carbohydrates: 52g | Fiber: 3g | Protein: 31g

Ginger-Lime Salmon

The slow cooker does all the work in this recipe, creating a healthy yet impressive dish that requires virtually no hands-on time.

INGREDIENTS | SERVES 12

1 3-pound salmon fillet, bones removed
¼ cup minced fresh ginger
¼ cup lime juice
1 lime, thinly sliced
1 onion, thinly sliced

Cracked!

Before each use, check your slow cooker for cracks. Even small cracks in the glaze can allow bacteria to grow in the ceramic insert. If there are cracks, replace the insert or the whole slow cooker.

1. Place the salmon skin-side down in an oval 6- to 7-quart slow cooker. Pour the ginger and lime juice over the fish. Arrange the lime and then the onion in single layers over the fish.

2. Cook on low for 3–4 hours or until the fish is fully cooked and flaky. Remove the skin before serving.

PER SERVING Calories: 170 | Fat: 7g | Sodium: 50mg | Carbohydrates: 2g | Fiber: 0g | Protein: 23g

CHAPTER 16

For Couples

Pineapple Pork Chops

Serve these sweet and hot chops with rice.

INGREDIENTS | SERVES 2

1 small onion, sliced

3 ¼"-thick fresh pineapple slices

½ pound thick-cut boneless pork chops

2 tablespoons soy sauce

1 teaspoon fresh ginger, grated

3 Thai bird peppers, minced

Substitution Suggestion

If you can't find Thai bird peppers or if you want a dish with less heat, substitute 1 jalapeño. Habanero peppers or Scotch bonnet peppers are quite hot and fruity tasting and would also make good substitutions. A tablespoon of hot sauce could be used in a pinch.

1. Place the onion slices on bottom of a 1½- to 2-quart slow cooker. Top with a pineapple slice. Center 1 pork chop over the pineapple slice. Top with a second pineapple slice. Center the second pork chop over the pineapple. Top with the last pineapple slice.

2. Add the soy sauce, ginger, and peppers. Cook on low for 8–10 hours.

PER SERVING Calories: 300 | Fat: 10g | Sodium: 1,080mg | Carbohydrates: 17g | Fiber: 2g | Protein: 37g

Chicken Taco Filling

Perfect for a quick weeknight meal, the preparation time is short and the spices get the entire day to flavor the meat.

INGREDIENTS | SERVES 2

1 small onion, diced

1 clove garlic, minced

2 tablespoons minced jalapeño

½ pound ground chicken

½ cup diced tomato

½ teaspoon ground chipotle

½ teaspoon oregano

¼ teaspoon hot paprika

½ teaspoon hot Mexican-style chili powder

½ teaspoon ground cayenne

1. In a small nonstick skillet, sauté the onions, garlic, jalapeño, and chicken until the chicken is cooked through, about 3 minutes. Drain off any grease.

2. Add the chicken mixture and the remaining ingredients to a 1½- to 2-quart slow cooker. Stir to incorporate the spices into the meat. Cook for 6–8 hours on low.

PER SERVING Calories: 180 | Fat: 9g | Sodium: 80mg | Carbohydrates: 7g | Fiber: 2g | Protein: 19g

What Is Chipotle?

Chipotle peppers are smoked jalapeño peppers. Their smoky hot flavor is perfect for adding depth and heat to slow-cooked foods. Chipotles are often found as a ground spice or in adobo, a tomato-onion sauce. They are also available as whole, dried peppers.

Twenty Cloves of Garlic Chicken

This is a scaled-down version of the classic dish Forty Cloves of Garlic Chicken.

INGREDIENTS | SERVES 2

20 whole cloves of garlic
1 split chicken breast
⅛ teaspoon salt
⅛ teaspoon black pepper

Cooking Tip

If you need to cook the chicken longer than the suggested 6–7 hours, add ¼ cup chicken broth to the slow cooker at the beginning of the cooking time. This will help keep the chicken juicy. Alternately, add half an onion.

1. Peel the garlic cloves. Sprinkle the chicken with salt and pepper.

2. Place the chicken breast and garlic cloves in a 1½- to 2-quart slow cooker. Cook on low for 6–7 hours.

PER SERVING Calories: 150 | Fat: 7g | Sodium: 190mg | Carbohydrates: 5g | Fiber: 0g | Protein: 16g

Slow-Cooked Pinto Beans

Pinto beans make a great side dish or vegetarian taco filling.

INGREDIENTS | SERVES 2

10 ounces canned pinto beans, drained and rinsed
1 small onion, diced
2 cloves garlic, minced
2 tablespoons diced fresh jalapeño
½ teaspoon hot Mexican-style chili powder
¼ teaspoon minced fresh thyme
¼ teaspoon ground cayenne
¼ teaspoon habanero hot sauce

1. Add all ingredients to a 1½- to 2-quart slow cooker. Stir.

2. Cook on low for 8 hours.

PER SERVING Calories: 150 | Fat: 1.5g | Sodium: 440mg | Carbohydrates: 27g | Fiber: 8g | Protein: 8g

Pork Tenderloin with Sweet and Savory Apples

The tart apples sweeten over the long cooking time and nearly melt into the pork.

INGREDIENTS | **SERVES 2**

⅛ teaspoon salt

¼ teaspoon freshly ground black pepper

¾–1 pound boneless pork tenderloin

½ cup sliced onions

5 fresh sage leaves

2 cups peeled, diced Granny Smith apples

Pork Tenderloin Tip

Lean, boneless pork tenderloin is often sold in very large packages containing 2 or more tenderloins, with a combined weight that is frequently over 15 pounds. As a result, it can be very expensive. Buy pork tenderloin on sale, and cut the meat into meal-sized portions. Label and freeze the portions until they are needed.

1. Sprinkle salt and pepper on the tenderloin. Place the onion slices on the bottom of a 1½- to 2-quart slow cooker. Add the tenderloin. Place the sage on top of the meat. Top with the diced apples.

2. Cover and cook on low for 8–10 hours.

PER SERVING Calories: 300 | Fat: 6g | Sodium: 230mg | Carbohydrates: 25g | Fiber: 5g | Protein: 36g

Pork and Tomatillo Burrito Filling

Serve with tomatoes, lettuce, and avocado in large tortillas.

INGREDIENTS | SERVES 2

½ pound boneless lean pork tenderloin roast
¾ cup diced tomatillos
¼ cup sliced onions
½ jalapeño, diced
1 tablespoon lime juice

1. Place all ingredients into a 2-quart slow cooker. Stir. Cook on low for 8–10 hours.

2. Use a fork to shred all of the contents. Toss to distribute the ingredients evenly.

PER SERVING Calories: 160 | Fat: 4.5g | Sodium: 60mg | Carbohydrates: 5g | Fiber: 1g | Protein: 24g

Quinoa with Chorizo

Try this as an alternative to rice.

INGREDIENTS | SERVES 2

¼ cup lean Spanish-style chorizo
¼ cup sliced onions
½ cup quinoa, rinsed
1 cup water

Sauté the chorizo and onions in a small nonstick saucepan until the onions are soft. Drain off any excess fat. Add to a 1½- to 2-quart slow cooker along with the quinoa and water. Cover and cook on low for 2 hours. Stir before serving.

PER SERVING Calories: 300 | Fat: 14g | Sodium: 380mg | Carbohydrates: 31g | Fiber: 3g | Protein: 13g

Quinoa Basics

Although quinoa is treated like a grain, it is actually an edible seed. It is very high in protein and contains a balanced set of essential amino acids, making it a particularly complete source of protein. Quinoa is also high in fiber, iron, and magnesium.

Turkey White Chili

This recipe creates a complete one-pot meal for two.

INGREDIENTS | SERVES 2

¼ cup drained canned hominy

¼ cup cooked or canned cannellini beans, drained and rinsed

¼ cup onions, diced

1 teaspoon lemon juice

½ teaspoon cumin

½ teaspoon paprika

½ teaspoon white pepper

2 ounces drained canned green peppers

½ cooked turkey breast, cubed

Place all ingredients except the turkey into a 2-quart slow cooker. Stir to mix the ingredients. Cook on low for 8 hours; stir in the turkey. Cook for an additional 30–60 minutes on high.

PER SERVING Calories: 110 | Fat: 1.5g | Sodium: 170mg | Carbohydrates: 11g | Fiber: 2g | Protein: 12g

Honey-Mustard Pork Loin

A mixture of mustard and honey keep the pork from drying out during the long cooking time.

INGREDIENTS | SERVES 2

3 tablespoon Dijon mustard

1 tablespoon mild honey

½ pound pork tenderloin

1. In a small bowl, mix the mustard and honey. Spread the mixture on the pork tenderloin in an even layer.

2. Place into a 2-quart slow cooker. Cook on low for 6 hours.

PER SERVING Calories: 200 | Fat: 6g | Sodium: 630mg | Carbohydrates: 11g | Fiber: 0g | Protein: 25g

Mexican Stuffed Peppers

This spicy twist on classic stuffed peppers is a great way to use up leftover chicken or turkey breast.

INGREDIENTS | SERVES 2

2 large poblano peppers
1 teaspoon canola oil
1 onion, diced
2 jalapeños, minced
¼ cup corn kernels
4 cloves garlic, minced
1 cup shredded cooked chicken or turkey breast
28 ounces canned crushed tomatoes

Suitable for Stuffing

Look for peppers that are plump, round, and not overly wrinkled. Peppers should not be bent over on themselves. You want large peppers for this recipe. Even without cutting them up, it should be clear that there is a large cavity inside.

1. Place the peppers on a broiler-safe tray. Broil on high for 2–5 minutes; flip and broil for 2–5 minutes on the other side. Rub each pepper with paper towels to remove the skin. Cut off the tops and cut a slit vertically down the middle of the pepper. Remove the seeds and discard them.

2. Heat the oil in a nonstick pan. Sauté the onions, jalapeños, corn, garlic, and meat until the onions are translucent.

3. Pour the meat mixture into a medium bowl. Stir in ¾ cup tomatoes. Divide the mixture and fill the peppers. "Close" the peppers by bringing both sides together.

4. Pour the remaining tomatoes onto the bottom of an oval 4-quart slow cooker. Top with the peppers. Cover and cook on low for 5 hours. Drizzle the sauce over the peppers prior to serving.

PER SERVING Calories: 370 | Fat: 8g | Sodium: 590mg | Carbohydrates: 52g | Fiber: 14g | Protein: 32g

Étouffée

Étouffée is a spicy, creamy Cajun dish that is always served over rice.

INGREDIENTS | **SERVES 2**

1½ tablespoons butter
1 tablespoon Creole seasoning
2 tablespoons flour
1 clove garlic, minced
½ cup diced onion
¼ cup diced celery
1 habanero pepper, minced
¾ cup water
1 teaspoon hot sauce
1 teaspoon Worcestershire sauce
1 small tomato, diced
½ teaspoon dried thyme
½ pound shrimp
1 tablespoon minced parsley
¼ cup diced green onion

1. Place the butter, Creole seasoning, and flour in a medium nonstick skillet. Cook 1 minute, stirring twice. Add the garlic, onion, celery, and habanero. Sauté until the mixture is golden. Add the water and bring to a boil. Cook, stirring occasionally, until the mixture has thickened.

2. Scrape the mixture into a 2-quart slow cooker and add the hot sauce, Worcestershire sauce, tomato, and thyme. Cook on low for 1–2 hours.

3. Add the shrimp, parsley, and green onion. Stir. Cook on high for about 20 minutes or until the shrimp is fully cooked. Stir before serving.

PER SERVING Calories: 260 | Fat: 11g | Sodium: 1,240mg | Carbohydrates: 16g | Fiber: 2g | Protein: 25g

Catfish Smothered in Onions

This simple Cajun-inspired dish is wonderful when paired with Stewed Okra (page 210).

INGREDIENTS | SERVES 2

½ teaspoon canola oil

2 onions, sliced

2 cloves garlic, minced

1 jalapeño, diced

2 catfish fillets

1 small tomato, diced

½ teaspoon hot sauce

½ teaspoon Creole seasoning

1. Heat the oil in a nonstick pan. Sauté the onions, garlic, and jalapeño until softened.

2. Place the catfish in a 2-quart slow cooker. Top with remaining ingredients. Cook on low for 2½ hours or until the fish is fully cooked through.

PER SERVING Calories: 300 | Fat: 13g | Sodium: 270mg | Carbohydrates: 17g | Fiber: 4g | Protein: 27g

Homemade Creole Seasoning

In a small bowl, whisk 1 tablespoon each of garlic powder, onion powder, dried oregano, dried basil, and ½ tablespoon each of freshly ground black pepper, white pepper, cayenne, celery seed, and paprika. Store in an airtight container up to 1 year.

Rhubarb Pulled Pork

Rhubarb adds a tartness that contrasts with the sweetness of the pork.

INGREDIENTS | **SERVES 2**

½ pound pork loin
½ cup chopped rhubarb
1 small onion, diced
1 tablespoon ginger preserves
1 tablespoon chili sauce

1. Quickly sear the pork on all sides in a nonstick skillet. Place into a 2-quart slow cooker. Add remaining ingredients. Cook on high for 5 hours.

2. Remove the pork from the slow cooker. Shred with a fork. Mash the rhubarb in the slow cooker with a potato masher until smooth. Add the pork back into the slow cooker and stir to distribute the sauce evenly.

PER SERVING Calories: 260 | Fat: 10g | Sodium: 310mg | Carbohydrates: 8g | Fiber: 1g | Protein: 34g

Filipino Chicken Adobo

Adobo is the unofficial dish of the Philippines. There are many variations, but they all have a pleasant sour-tart flavor.

INGREDIENTS | **SERVES 2**

2 boneless, skinless chicken thighs
¼ cup water
¼ cup cane vinegar
¼ cup soy sauce
1 teaspoon whole black peppercorns
5 cloves garlic, halved
2 bay leaves

Place all ingredients in a 2-quart slow cooker. Cook for 6–8 hours. Discard the bay leaves before serving.

PER SERVING Calories: 150 | Fat: 6g | Sodium: 2,060mg | Carbohydrates: 7g | Fiber: <1g | Protein: 18g

Moroccan Lamb Stew

Look for boneless, lean lamb chops to dice for this recipe; it is cheaper and easier than buying a whole leg of lamb.

INGREDIENTS | SERVES 2

½ pound lean boneless lamb, cubed
2 cloves garlic, minced
½ onion, chopped
2 tablespoons lemon juice
¼ cup sliced green olives
2 teaspoons honey
¼ teaspoon salt
½ teaspoon freshly ground black pepper
¼ teaspoon turmeric
2 springs fresh thyme

Place the lamb, garlic, onion, lemon juice, olives, honey, salt, pepper, and turmeric in a 2-quart slow cooker. Top with the sprigs of thyme. Cook on low for 8 hours. Remove sprigs before serving.

PER SERVING Calories: 280 | Fat: 11g | Sodium: 630mg | Carbohydrates: 13g | Fiber: 2g | Protein: 32g

Ginger-Glazed Cornish Game Hen

The flavors of ginger and lime penetrate the meat, so you don't need to eat the skin to get the flavor.

INGREDIENTS | SERVES 2

4-pound Cornish game hen
2 tablespoons ginger powder
2 tablespoons fresh lime juice

Place the Cornish game hen in a 2-quart slow cooker. In a small bowl, whisk the ginger powder and lime juice. Pour over the hen. Cook on low for 6–7 hours. Discard the skin before serving.

PER SERVING Calories: 140 | Fat: 3.5g | Sodium: 55mg | Carbohydrates: 5g | Fiber: <1g | Protein: 21g

What Is a Cornish Game Hen?

The Cornish game hen first became available in the United States during the 1960s. Although the hen is often considered a separate kind of poultry, it is actually a small chicken. One large hen is perfect for two people, while a smaller 1- to 2-pound bird would be perfect for one.

Salmon with Lemon, Capers, and Rosemary

Salmon is very moist and tender when cooked in the slow cooker.

INGREDIENTS | **SERVES 2**

8 ounces salmon

⅓ cup water

2 tablespoons lemon juice

3 thin slices fresh lemon

1 tablespoon nonpareil capers

½ teaspoon minced fresh rosemary

1. Place the salmon on the bottom of a 2-quart slow cooker. Pour the water and lemon juice over the fish. Arrange the lemon slices in a single layer on top of the fish. Sprinkle with capers and rosemary.

2. Cook on low for 2 hours. Discard lemon slices prior to serving.

PER SERVING Calories: 170 | Fat: 7g | Sodium: 180mg | Carbohydrates: 2g | Fiber: 0g | Protein: 23g

Slow-Cooked Oatmeal with Dried and Fresh Fruit

Wake up to the perfect hearty breakfast for a chilly fall morning.

INGREDIENTS | **SERVES 2**

1 Bosc pear, peeled and cubed

1¼ cups water

¾ cup old-fashioned rolled oats

¼ cup dried tart cherries

¼ teaspoon sugar

¼ teaspoon ground ginger

Place all ingredients into a 2-quart slow cooker. Cook on low for 8 hours. Stir prior to serving.

PER SERVING Calories: 260 | Fat: 3g | Sodium: 0mg | Carbohydrates: 52g | Fiber: 7g | Protein: 6g

Winter Vegetable Soup

Flavorful root vegetables make this filling soup a delicious treat after a long, cold day.

1 small carrot, diced
1 stalk celery, diced
1 parsnip, diced
¼ cup cubed celeriac
¼ cup canned diced tomatoes
1 clove garlic, minced
1 shallot, minced
2 cups Chicken Stock (page 17)
1 teaspoon celery flakes
¼ teaspoon white pepper
⅛ teaspoon salt

Place all ingredients in a 2-quart slow cooker. Stir. Cook on low for 8 hours.

PER SERVING Calories: 210 | Fat: 3.5g | Sodium: 610mg | Carbohydrates: 38g | Fiber: 6g | Protein: 10g

Making Sense of Celeriac

Celeriac, also known as celery root or knob celery, is not a type of celery but is similar to celery in flavor. It has an unusually rough and knobby exterior and is about the size of a softball. Celeriac can be used cooked or raw, but it must be peeled before eating.

Beef Stroganoff

Slimmed-down comfort food for two. Serve over yolk-free egg noodles.

INGREDIENTS | SERVES 2

8 ounces lean bottom round, cubed

1½ tablespoons flour

1 small onion, diced

2 ounces sliced button or crimini mushrooms

⅛ teaspoon salt

¼ teaspoon freshly ground pepper

2 cloves garlic, minced

¼ cup reduced-fat sour cream

1. Toss the beef in the flour. Add it to a 2-quart slow cooker. Add the onion, mushrooms, salt, pepper, and garlic.

2. Cook on low for 8 hours. Stir in sour cream and serve.

PER SERVING Calories: 310 | Fat: 17g | Sodium: 220mg | Carbohydrates: 12g | Fiber: <1g | Protein: 26g

Salt and Slow Cooking

Salt helps bring out the flavor in both savory and sweet dishes, but be careful when you're slow cooking. Always err on the side of using too little; the long cooking time can intensify the flavor. If a dish needs salt, add it at the end.

Cuban Picadillo

In Cuba, picadillo is served with black beans and rice.

INGREDIENTS | SERVES 2

8 ounces 94% lean ground beef
¼ cup diced tomato
¼ cup pimento-stuffed green olives
½ tablespoon nonpareil capers
1 shallot minced
½ tablespoon tomato paste
¼ teaspoon cumin
⅛ teaspoon freshly ground black pepper
⅛ teaspoon salt

1. In a small, nonstick skillet, sauté the beef until cooked through. Break up large pieces with the back of a spoon.

2. Add the meat and remaining ingredients to a 2-quart slow cooker. Stir to distribute all ingredients evenly. Cook on low for 6–8 hours. Stir prior to serving.

PER SERVING Calories: 240 | Fat: 10g | Sodium: 810mg | Carbohydrates: 11g | Fiber: <1g | Protein: 26g

Why Use Freshly Ground Pepper?

Freshly ground pepper has a fresher, spicier flavor than ground pepper. To keep it free flowing, ground pepper is often packaged with fillers that can dull the flavor. Whole peppercorns take just seconds to grind in a peppermill.

Roast Beef

Couples deserve a good roast dinner just as much as larger families.
So enjoy this one without having to eat leftovers for a week.

INGREDIENTS | **SERVES 2**

½ teaspoon freshly ground black pepper

½ teaspoon fennel seeds

½ teaspoon crushed rosemary

¼ teaspoon salt

½ teaspoon dried oregano

¾ pound bottom round roast, excess fat removed

¼ cup Caramelized Onions (page 16)

¼ cup water or beef stock

1 clove garlic, sliced

1. In a small bowl, stir the pepper, fennel seeds, rosemary, salt, and oregano. Rub it into all sides of the meat. Refrigerate for 15 minutes.

2. Place the roast in a 2-quart slow cooker. Add the onions, water or stock, and garlic. Cook on low for 8 hours. Remove and slice. Serve topped with the Caramelized Onions. Discard any cooking juices.

PER SERVING Calories: 340 | Fat: 20g | Sodium: 390mg | Carbohydrates: 2g | Fiber: <1g | Protein: 36g

CHAPTER 17

Desserts

Coconut Rice Pudding

Evaporated milk gives this rice pudding an amazingly creamy texture without the fat of whole milk or cream.

INGREDIENTS | SERVES 8

¾ cup long-grain rice

3½ cups fat-free evaporated milk

⅔ cup sugar

⅓ cup unsweetened shredded coconut

½ teaspoon vanilla

¼ teaspoon salt

¼ teaspoon orange peel

Place all ingredients into a 4-quart slow cooker. Stir. Cook on low for 5 hours. Stir before serving.

PER SERVING Calories: 240 | Fat: 3g | Sodium: 200mg | Carbohydrates: 44g | Fiber: <1g | Protein: 10g

Quick Tip

Rice pudding has a tendency to thicken as it cools. If you want a looser, creamier texture, stir in a bit of water to each bowl before serving. Reheat leftovers for optimum flavor and texture.

Strawberry Pandowdy

The pandowdy gets its name from the dowdy appearance that is achieved by breaking up the crust halfway through the cooking time to allow the juices to soak through.

INGREDIENTS | SERVES 4

4 cups whole strawberries, stems removed

½ teaspoon ground ginger

1½ tablespoons sugar

½ teaspoon cornstarch

¾ cup flour

3 tablespoons cold butter, cubed

3 tablespoons cold water

⅛ teaspoon salt

What's the Difference Between a Betty, a Cobbler, a Pandowdy, and a Slump?

A betty is a baked dish made by alternating layers of spiced, sugared fruit and buttered bread crumbs. A cobbler is a fruit stew in which biscuit dough is dropped onto the fruit before cooking. A pandowdy is a spoon pie with fruit on the bottom and a rolled pie crust on top that is broken up halfway through the cooking time. A slump is a spoon pie as well that includes cooked fruit topped with biscuit dough.

1. Place the strawberries, ginger, sugar, and cornstarch into a 2-quart slow cooker. Toss to distribute evenly.

2. Place the flour, butter, water, and salt into a food processor. Mix until a solid ball of dough forms. Roll it out on a clean surface until it is about ¼"–½" thick and will completely cover the fruit in the insert.

3. Drape the dough over the strawberries. Cover and cook on high for 40 minutes. Remove the lid. Using the tip of a knife, cut the dough into 2" squares without removing it from the slow cooker. Keep the lid off and continue to cook on high for an additional 40 minutes. Serve hot.

PER SERVING Calories: 230 | Fat: 9g | Sodium: 75mg | Carbohydrates: 34g | Fiber: 4g | Protein: 3g

Green Tea Tapioca Pudding

Tapioca pudding is simple in the slow cooker. There's no need to stir!

INGREDIENTS | SERVES 6

2 cups fat-free evaporated milk

¼ cup small pearl tapioca

1 teaspoon matcha or green tea powder

½ cup sugar

1 egg

Tapioca

Tapioca comes in several forms. Large pearl tapioca can be boiled to a chewy texture and served Taiwanese-style in cold drinks. Small pearl tapioca is better used in puddings and desserts. Tapioca starch is also used as a thickener in savory dishes.

1. Pour the evaporated milk, tapioca, matcha, and sugar into a 4-quart slow cooker. Whisk until the sugar dissolves. Cook for 1½ hours.

2. Stir in the egg. Cook an additional ½ hour on low. Serve warm.

PER SERVING Calories: 170 | Fat: 1g | Sodium: 110mg | Carbohydrates: 32g | Fiber: 0g | Protein: 8g

Slow-Cooked Pineapple

Slow cooking makes pineapple meltingly tender. Serve as-is or with vanilla bean frozen yogurt.

INGREDIENTS | SERVES 8

1 whole pineapple, peeled

1 vanilla bean, split

3 tablespoons water or rum

Cooking with Vanilla Beans

Vanilla beans have a natural "seam" that can easily be split to release the flavorful seeds inside. After using a vanilla bean, wash it and allow it to dry. Then place it in a container with a few cups of sugar for a few weeks to make vanilla sugar.

Place all ingredients into a 4-quart oval slow cooker. Cook on low for 4 hours or until fork tender. Remove the vanilla bean before serving.

PER SERVING Calories: 35 | Fat: 0g | Sodium: 0mg | Carbohydrates: 8g | Fiber: <1g | Protein: 0g

Berry Cobbler

Try this with a mix of blackberries, raspberries, golden raspberries, and blueberries.
If the berries are very tart, add an extra tablespoon of sugar.

INGREDIENTS	SERVES 8

4 cups mixed fresh berries
2½ tablespoons brown sugar
3 tablespoons minced fresh mint
1 cup flour
1½ tablespoons sugar
½ teaspoon ground ginger
1 egg
¼ cup fat-free evaporated milk
1½ tablespoons canola oil

Keep Your Berries Well

Berries are very fragile. For the best flavor, leave them out at room temperature rather than in the refrigerator. Avoid bruising berries by washing them directly before use. Buy local berries and eat them as soon as possible to avoid spoilage.

1. Toss the berries, brown sugar, and mint. Set aside.

2. Whisk the dry ingredients in a medium bowl. Beat in the egg, evaporated milk, and oil until a thick dough forms.

3. Spray a 4-quart slow cooker with cooking spray. Spread the dough along the bottom, taking care to cover the entire bottom with no gaps. Add the berries in an even layer.

4. Cook on low for 2 hours.

PER SERVING Calories: 150 | Fat: 3.5g | Sodium: 20mg | Carbohydrates: 27g | Fiber: 3g | Protein: 4g

Challah Bread Pudding

This slimmed-down bread pudding is a wonderful way to use up leftover, even slightly stale, challah.

INGREDIENTS | SERVES 10

4 cups cubed challah

⅓ cup dried tart cherries or cranberries

2⅓ cups fat-free evaporated milk

2 eggs

⅓ cup dark brown sugar

1 teaspoon vanilla extract

1 teaspoon cinnamon

½ teaspoon ground ginger

¼ teaspoon nutmeg

1. Spray a 4-quart slow cooker with cooking spray. Add the bread cubes and dried fruit. Stir.

2. In a medium bowl, whisk the evaporated milk, eggs, brown sugar, vanilla, cinnamon, ginger, and nutmeg. Pour over the bread crumbs and dried fruit.

3. Cook for 5 hours on low or until the pudding no longer looks liquid.

PER SERVING Calories: 140 | Fat: 2g | Sodium: 150mg | Carbohydrates: 24g | Fiber: <1g | Protein: 7g

Breaking Bread

It is important to cut the bread used for bread pudding into uniform 1"–2" cubes for maximum absorption and distribution of liquid. Slightly stale bread cuts easily and can be used in bread puddings or stuffing. Bread cubes can even be frozen for future use.

Cheesecake

Making cheesecake in the slow cooker might sound odd, but it is actually the perfect appliance for the job. The constant low heat and moist environment keeps it from drying out or cracking, even when using low-fat ingredients.

INGREDIENTS | SERVES 8

¾ cup low-fat chocolate or cinnamon graham cracker crumbs

1½ tablespoons butter, melted

8 ounces reduced-fat sour cream, at room temperature

8 ounces reduced-fat cream cheese, at room temperature

⅔ cup sugar

1 egg, at room temperature

1 tablespoon vanilla paste or vanilla extract

1½ tablespoons flour

1 tablespoon lemon juice

1 tablespoon lemon zest

Homemade Graham Cracker Crumbs

There is no need to buy packaged graham cracker crumbs, it is easy to make them at home. Break graham crackers into medium-sized pieces. Place them into a food processor. Pulse until fine crumbs form. Store the crumbs in an airtight container.

1. In a small bowl, mix together the graham cracker crumbs and butter. Press into the bottom and sides of a 6" springform pan.

2. In a large bowl, mix the sour cream, cream cheese, sugar, egg, vanilla, flour, lemon juice, and zest until completely smooth. Pour into the springform pan.

3. Pour 1" of water into the bottom of a 6-quart slow cooker. Place a trivet in the bottom of the slow cooker. Place the pan onto the trivet.

4. Cook on low for 2 hours. Turn off the slow cooker and let the cheesecake steam for 1 hour and 15 minutes with the lid on. Remove the cheesecake from the slow cooker. Refrigerate 6 hours or overnight before serving.

PER SERVING Calories: 240 | Fat: 12g | Sodium: 150mg | Carbohydrates: 28g | Fiber: 0g | Protein: 5g

Pear and Cranberry Crumble

Pears and cranberries make a sweet-tart base for this homey crumble.

INGREDIENTS | SERVES 6

3 Bosc pears, thinly sliced

¾ cup fresh cranberries

2 tablespoons light brown sugar

2 tablespoons melted unsalted butter

½ cup old-fashioned rolled oats

⅛ cup flour

½ teaspoon cinnamon

⅛ teaspoon nutmeg

½ tablespoon sugar

1. Spray a 2-quart slow cooker with nonstick spray. Add the pears, cranberries, and brown sugar. Stir. Cook for 3 hours on high.

2. In a small bowl, whisk the butter, oats, flour, cinnamon, nutmeg, and sugar. Sprinkle over the fruit and cook on high for 30 minutes. Remove the lid and cook an additional 10 minutes on high, uncovered.

PER SERVING Calories: 150 | Fat: 4.5g | Sodium: 0mg | Carbohydrates: 26g | Fiber: 4g | Protein: 2g

Appealing Pears

Perhaps the most common variety of pear is the Bartlett. Sweet and juicy, it comes in both red and green variations. Bosc pears are uniformly brown and have a dull skin. Their denser texture makes them perfect for baking or slow cooking.

Chocolate Bread Pudding

*Fat-free evaporated milk gives this bread pudding a creamy texture,
but it has several dozen fewer calories than heavy cream.*

INGREDIENTS | SERVES 10

4 cups cubed Italian bread

2⅓ cups fat-free evaporated milk

2 eggs

⅓ cup light brown sugar

¼ cup cocoa

1 teaspoon vanilla extract

Suggested Bread Pudding Variations

Instead of white bread, use a mixture of white and whole wheat. Or add ½ cup coconut to the bread cubes. Or add ⅓ cup raisins or a mixture of dried fruit to the bread cubes. Or scrape a vanilla bean into the milk mixture for extra vanilla flavor.

1. Spray a 4-quart slow cooker with cooking spray. Add the bread cubes.

2. In a medium bowl, whisk the evaporated milk, eggs, brown sugar, cocoa, and vanilla until the sugar and cocoa dissolve. Pour over the bread cubes.

3. Cook for 5 hours on low or until the pudding no longer looks liquid.

PER SERVING Calories: 130 | Fat: 2g | Sodium: 170mg | Carbohydrates: 22g | Fiber: 1g | Protein: 7g

Apple Brown Betty

Apple Brown Betty is an American dessert that dates back to colonial times.

INGREDIENTS | SERVES 6

3½ cups cubed apples
1 tablespoon lemon juice
1 tablespoon sugar
½ teaspoon cinnamon
½ teaspoon ground ginger
¼ teaspoon nutmeg
¼ teaspoon allspice
1¾ cups bread cubes

Lemon Juice

Lemon juice is a cook's best friend. It adds a bright note to most dishes. It is low in calories but high in vitamin C. It can even keep cut apples or pears from turning brown.

1. Spray a 2-quart slow cooker with nonstick spray. Add the apples, lemon juice, sugar, and spices. Stir. Cook on high 2 hours.

2. Preheat oven to 250°F. Spread the bread cubes in a single layer on a baking sheet. Bake until browned, about 8 minutes.

3. Sprinkle the toasted bread cubes over the apples. Cook on high for 10 minutes prior to serving.

PER SERVING Calories: 80 | Fat: 0.5g | Sodium: 70mg | Carbohydrates: 18g | Fiber: 2g | Protein: 1g

Light and Creamy Hot Fudge Sauce

Try this over frozen yogurt or ice cream.

INGREDIENTS | **YIELDS 2 CUPS (ABOUT 30 SERVINGS)**

12 ounces fat-free evaporated milk

10 ounces semisweet or bittersweet chocolate chips

1 teaspoon vanilla

½ teaspoon butter

⅛ teaspoon salt

1. Place all ingredients in a 1½- to 2-quart slow cooker. Cook on low, stirring occasionally for 2 hours. The sauce will thicken as it cools.

2. Refrigerate leftovers. Reheat in the slow cooker for 1 hour on high or on the stovetop until warmed through, about 10 minutes.

PER SERVING | Calories: 60 | Fat: 3g | Sodium: 25mg | Carbohydrates: 7g | Fiber: <1g | Protein: 1g

Orange-Scented Custard

Orange blossom water is a common Middle Eastern ingredient that adds a fruity, floral note to this custard.

INGREDIENTS | **SERVES 10**

1 tablespoon orange blossom water, or ½ teaspoon orange extract

2 cups fat-free evaporated milk

5 eggs

⅓ cup sugar

Place all ingredients into a large bowl. Whisk until smooth. Pour into a 4-quart slow cooker. Cook on low for 8 hours, or until the center looks set and does not jiggle.

PER SERVING Calories: 100 | Fat: 2.5g | Sodium: 95mg | Carbohydrates: 13g | Fiber: 0g | Protein: 7g

Chocolate Crème Brûlée

This elegant dessert can be cooking away all through dinner.

INGREDIENTS | SERVES 4

2 cups fat-free evaporated milk

2½ tablespoons cocoa

½ teaspoon vanilla extract

4 egg yolks

½ cup sugar

2 tablespoons brown sugar

Vanilla Extract Is Essential

When a recipe calls for vanilla, use real vanilla extract. Although real vanilla extract is more expensive than imitation, the flavor is far superior. Store vanilla extract in a cool, dark place to preserve the flavor.

1. In a small bowl, whisk the evaporated milk, cocoa, vanilla, egg yolks, and sugar until the sugar dissolves. Pour the mixture into a small pan and bring it to a boil. Remove the pan from the heat and allow the mixture to cool. Divide it among four 5- to 6-ounce broiler-safe ramekins.

2. Pour 1" of water into the bottom of an oval 6-quart slow cooker. Place the ramekins in the water. Cook on high for 3 hours or until the custard is set.

3. Sprinkle each Crème Brûlée with ½ tablespoon brown sugar. Place them under the broiler and broil until the sugar caramelizes.

PER SERVING Calories: 290 | Fat: 5g | Sodium: 160mg | Carbohydrates: 49g | Fiber: 1g | Protein: 13g

Chai Pudding

Any tea lover would delight in this creamy tapioca pudding.

INGREDIENTS | SERVES 6

2 chai tea bags

2 cups fat-free evaporated milk

⅓ cup brown sugar

½ teaspoon cinnamon

½ teaspoon ground star anise

½ teaspoon mace

½ teaspoon ground cardamom

¼ cup small pearl tapioca

1 egg

1. Steep the tea bags in the evaporated milk for 20 minutes. Discard the bags. Whisk in the sugar, spices, and tapioca.

2. Pour the mixture into a 2- or 4-quart slow cooker and cook on low for 1½ hours. Stir in the egg and continue to cook for 30 minutes.

PER SERVING Calories: 150 | Fat: 1g | Sodium: 115mg | Carbohydrates: 28g | Fiber: 0g | Protein: 8g

Vanilla Poached Pears

Slow poaching makes these pears meltingly tender and infuses them with a rich vanilla flavor.

INGREDIENTS | SERVES 4

4 Bosc pears, peeled

1 vanilla bean, split

2 tablespoons vanilla extract

2 cups water

Stand the pears up in a 4-quart oval slow cooker. Add the remaining ingredients. Cook on low for 2 hours or until the pears are tender. Discard all cooking liquid prior to serving.

PER SERVING Calories: 100 | Fat: 0g | Sodium: 0mg | Carbohydrates: 22g | Fiber: 4g | Protein: 1g

Caramel Popcorn

The slow cooker provides an easy way to make caramel without a lot of hands-on time. If it is very thick, thin it out with a few tablespoons of water.

INGREDIENTS | SERVES 12

1½ cups light brown sugar

2 tablespoons butter, cubed

8 quarts air-popped popcorn

Popcorn Facts

Popcorn is an excellent source of fiber. It is a healthy choice for a snack, especially if it is popped in an air popper without any added fat. Drizzle with a small amount of caramel sauce for a sweet treat or sprinkle with Parmesan for a savory snack.

1. Place the sugar and butter into a 4-quart slow cooker. Cook for 1 hour on high, stirring occasionally, until caramel forms.

2. Drizzle over popcorn and toss. Serve immediately.

PER SERVING Calories: 200 | Fat: 3g | Sodium: 25mg | Carbohydrates: 43g | Fiber: 3g | Protein: 3g

Summer Berry Slump

A slump is a fruit dessert served with fresh, steamed dumplings.

INGREDIENTS | **SERVES 8**

4 cups mixed fresh berries
1½ tablespoons sugar
1 teaspoon minced fresh ginger
1 cup flour
½ teaspoon ground ginger
1 egg
¼ cup fat-free evaporated milk
1½ tablespoons canola oil

1. Toss the berries, sugar, and fresh ginger together. Set aside.

2. Whisk the dry ingredients in a medium bowl. Beat in the egg, evaporated milk, and canola oil until a thick dough forms. Shape into 2" dumplings.

3. Spray a 4-quart slow cooker with cooking spray. Add the berries in an even layer. Drop in the dumplings.

4. Cook on low for 2 hours.

PER SERVING Calories: 140 | Fat: 3.5g | Sodium: 20mg | Carbohydrates: 23g | Fiber: 3g | Protein: 4g

Healthy Slow-Cooking Tips

Here's how to avoid falling into the high-fat, high-calorie slow-cooking trap.

- Instead of using creamy, high-fat, high-sodium condensed soups, use fat-free evaporated milk or fat-free, sodium-free stocks.

- Leave the skin on potatoes, apples, and pears for extra fiber.

- Add dried fruits to hot cereals at the beginning of the cooking time for a burst of flavor and healthful fiber.

- Use only lean cuts of meat.

- Add beans to a dish for extra protein and fiber.

- Use low-sodium versions of canned tomatoes, beans, and chiles.

- Remember that brightly colored fruits and vegetables have more vitamins and nutrients than their paler counterparts.

- Use nonstick cookware when browning meat to avoid adding extra fat.

- Eat fruits and vegetables that are in season whenever possible. Not only will they be cheaper, they will be at the height of their flavor and nutritional value.

- Adding just one extra serving of fruits or vegetables to each meal can have enormous health benefits.

- Add spices for flavor instead of adding fat.

- Use low- or reduced-fat versions of dairy products to "lighten up" meals.

- Thoroughly drain the fat off any cooked, browned, or seared meat prior to adding it to the slow cooker.

- Poultry skin becomes unappetizingly rubbery when cooked in the slow cooker. Remove it before or after cooking to save calories.

How to Make Your Favorite Recipes Lower in Fat

The following are easy substitutions and tips for making meals healthily in the slow cooker without sacrificing flavor.

- Choose lean cuts of meat and use only 94 percent lean ground beef, pork, turkey, and chicken.

- Remove any visible fat from meats prior to adding them to the slow cooker.

- Brown meats and drain off the grease before slow cooking.

- Use fat-free evaporated milk instead of heavy cream or whole milk.

- Make your own sauces using evaporated milk or broth instead of using canned soup.

- Use less butter or oil and more herbs and spices.

- Low-fat versions of cream cheese, sour cream, mayonnaise, and cheese work well in the slow cooker.

- Sticking is not an issue in the slow cooker, so at least halve the amount of butter or oil in a traditional recipe to convert it to slow cooking.

- Use lots of fresh, fiber-rich fruits, vegetables, and legumes to leave you feeling full with little or no fat needed.

- Use cooking spray instead of butter or oil to grease the slow cooker insert or skillets.

Resources

These lists highlight one-stop spots for health and cookware information.

Health Information

Beefitswhatsfordinner.com

This page contains an informative chart showing the nutritional profile of lean beef and how certain cuts compare to boneless skinless chicken breasts and thighs.

www.3beefitswhatsfordinner.com/leanbeef.aspx

FoodSafety.gov

Helpful tips and links about food safety.

www.foodsafety.gov

MyPyramid.gov

This website offers personalized eating plans and tools to customize your food choices.

www.mypyramid.gov

Porkandhealth.org

This website is great source for nutritional information on pork products, including charts of which cuts are the leanest.

www.porkandhealth.org

Seasonal Ingredient Map

This interactive map shows you what foods are currently in season in your area.

www.epicurious.com/articlesguides/seasonalcooking/farmtotable/seasonalingredientmap

Equipment Sources

Chicago Metallic Bakeware

This site offers a wide range of nonstick cookware.

🖰 *www.cmbakeware.com*

Cuisinart

Probably best known for their innovative food processors, Cuisinart also has a wide selection of countertop appliances and cookware.

🖰 *www.cuisinart.com*

General Electric

Slow cookers

🖰 *www.gehousewares.com*

Hamilton Beach

Slow cookers

🖰 *www.hamiltonbeach.com*

Kaiser Bakeware

Baking sheets

🖰 *www.kaiserbakeware.com*

Reynolds Consumer Products Company

Reynolds Slow Cooker Liners

🖰 *www.reynoldskitchens.com*

Rival

Slow cookers

🖰 *www.crock-pot.com*

Taylor Precision Products LP

Taylor Digital Oven Thermometer/Timer

🖰 *www.taylorusa.com*

Index